Decadent
Vegan Cakes

Decadent

Vegan Cakes

Outstanding Plant-Based Recipes for Layer Cakes,
Sheet Cakes, Cupcakes and More

CHARLOTTE ROBERTS

Creator of Charley's Health

PAGE STREET
PUBLISHING CO.

First published in 2023 by
Page Street Publishing Co.
27 Congress Street, Suite 105
Salem, MA 01970
www.pagestreetpublishing.com

Distributed by Macmillan, sales in Canada by The Canadian Manda Group.

27   26   25   24   23   1   2   3   4   5

ISBN-13: 978-1-64567-975-2
ISBN-10: 1-64567-975-6

Library of Congress Control Number: 2022946825

Cover and book design by Rosie Stewart for Page Street Publishing Co.
Photography by Charlotte Roberts

Printed and bound in the United States

DEDICATION

I want to dedicate this book to everyone who has followed and supported my journey and Charley's Health. I'm so thankful for all of you and for the opportunity to bring you my first cookbook! I hope you enjoy making, eating and sharing these recipes as much as I do!

Table of Contents

LOAF & BUNDT CAKES   117

CELEBRATION & OCCASION CAKES   137

Introduction

Food plays a huge role in our lives, aside from simply feeding us. Whether it be in the simple everyday meal or celebratory occasions, eating is an experience to be enjoyed with others. I think that I'm especially fond of making desserts, as they're something almost everyone enjoys, and I firmly believe that a little bite of indulgence is an excellent way to finish off any meal! I've also completely fallen in love with the process of experimenting and creating them, as well as then being able to share and bring joy to friends and family. There's something quite special about taking that little bit of extra time and effort to prepare a treat that you know will bring happiness to other people and help create special memories!

My mission through my blog, and now this book, is to show you how easily you can adapt your favorite desserts for plant-based options, as well as proving that this doesn't mean compromising on taste. Whether you're catering for a vegan friend, following a plant-based diet or looking for a cookbook to introduce people to vegan recipes, dessert is a tasty place to start.

What initially sparked my interest in vegan baking was the challenge of creating plant-based alternatives to classic favorites and experimenting with different ingredient swaps.

I've always found a common misconception around vegan baking is that you're going to be heavily compromising on taste or that it's going to involve a rather complicated process. I know I've sampled my fair share of dry, crumbly free-from cakes, which is something I am determined to prove is not inevitable. I aim to make vegan baking easy and accessible, so you'll be able to enjoy all your favorite classic cakes and try some new ones, too.

Something else that is key to making incredible dishes in the kitchen is creativity. Although baking is a culinary art that requires recipes to be followed meticulously and scientifically, I always encourage people to add their own individual touches. Each of my cake recipes include its accompanying frosting and topping suggestions with step-by-step instructions. While these are my personal favorite pairings, many of my cakes and frostings are interchangeable. I encourage you to let your creativity run wild and try different mix-and-match combinations.

I've tried my best to make sure that there is something in this book to suit everyone's tastes and all occasions. So, whether you're looking for a simple one-pan bake, breakfast loaf cake, classic chocolate birthday cake or an extravagant seasonal showstopper, this will be your ultimate vegan cake guide!

Charley

Vegan Baking Shopping List

Throughout the book, you'll probably notice that many of the recipes use some of the same ingredients, which make up my core collection of baking cupboard staples. Most of these items are readily available at local grocery stores and are also fairly inexpensive. This is something that was important to me when developing these recipes, as I wanted them to be widely accessible and as affordable as I could make them. I know that baking decadent layer cakes can be on the expensive side, but the core ingredients are versatile and can be used over again in other recipes.

I've followed many a recipe that has led me to buying weird and wonderful ingredients, only for them to end up at the back of my kitchen cupboards after a single use. I didn't want that to be the case with these recipes, so I have made sure the following ingredients can be used regularly. Some are ingredients required in everyday baking and others are specific to transforming your cakes into plant-based alternatives.

VEGAN STICK BUTTER

You will notice that most of the frosting recipes call for vegan stick butter, so it's helpful to always have a couple of sticks on hand in the fridge. When making vegan buttercream frosting, it's important that you use stick butter instead of a nondairy spread, as this will help to create that thick, creamy consistency. The quantities of butter and sugar will not be the same if you use a spread, so the correct texture won't be guaranteed.

NONDAIRY MILK

I'm sure nondairy milk is something that you will always have on hand and is required for pretty much every recipe in the book. My preferred milk to use when baking is soy milk, as I find it works best to create vegan buttermilk. For most of my cake recipes, the instructions call for combining apple cider vinegar with your plant-based milk, which thickens it and forms a buttermilk replacement. This is a great dairy-free baking hack and can also work using lemon juice instead of vinegar.

SELF-RISING FLOUR

Generally speaking, I like to use self-rising flour for my vegan bakes, as it helps to create a light and fluffy sponge-cake texture and always achieves the perfect rise! I use regular self-rising flour, so if you do follow a gluten-free diet, then you would need to try switching these for a 1:1 gluten-free flour blend.

OLIVE OIL

As well as plant-based butters, olive oil is an ingredient I love using in my baking, as I adore the fluffy texture it creates. When selecting an olive oil for baking, I always try to find one that's light in color with a mild flavor. This is important because you don't want any bitter flavors over-powering the flavor of your cake! Similarly, if you're baking a pale sponge cake, using a darker colored oil could affect the finish.

SUGAR

Sugar is a predictable and self-explanatory staple, so I'll keep things brief. I use three main kinds of sugar most frequently in my recipes: granulated sugar, light brown sugar and powdered sugar. Granulated sugar is my choice for general cake making, brown sugar for chocolate bakes and for a slightly richer flavor or caramel sauces and powdered sugar for frostings.

CHICKPEA WATER

A slightly more unexpected baking staple, but incredibly useful and effective: chickpea water. This is also known as aquafaba and is what's used to make vegan meringues. Aquafaba is a great way to not only utilize the water from your chickpea cans but also allow you to make incredible meringue frostings for your cakes . . . without any eggs!

HIGH-QUALITY COCOA POWDER

Just as there should be, there are a fair few chocolate-heavy recipes to be found in this book! For these, I always recommend finding yourself a good-quality cocoa or cacao powder to achieve a rich, luxurious flavor. I don't know about you, but if I'm making something chocolaty, then I'm looking for that truly indulgent, decadent chocolate taste!

PLANT-BASED YOGURT

Another staple used in so many of my recipes is a nondairy yogurt. My personal favorites are soy and coconut varieties. This is something that I've only started frequently incorporating into my baking over the last year or so, and I can honestly say that it's made a positive difference. The addition of yogurt helps to bind the ingredients together and keeps your sponge cakes perfectly moist!

Classic Flavors

I wanted to make sure that vegan baking never limited me from enjoying my all-time favorite cakes from my childhood, so this chapter is dedicated to classic flavor favorites.

What better way to demonstrate just how easily you can create incredible vegan cakes, without ever compromising on taste, than with these timeless flavors? I've filled this chapter with a selection of nostalgic cakes that have been my go-tos for any occasion, from large celebrations to casual afternoon teas. Each of these cakes, which have now been given a plant-based twist, bring back memories of delicious desserts enjoyed with friends and family.

Something I love about vegan baking is the opportunity to re-create well-loved dishes and produce something to rival the original recipes! I want to show you how easy it is to achieve those light and fluffy bakes that are both dairy- and egg-free, with just a few simple ingredient swaps. Whether you're hosting vegan friends or it's your turn to bring dessert, this chapter includes something that everyone will love!

I would, of course, recommend giving each one of these recipes a try. However, if I had to choose just one, it would be the Lemon Curd & Poppyseed Cake (page 27). This gives a decadent twist to a classic lemon and poppyseed recipe by adding a luxurious layer of plant-based lemon curd. It's perfect for all occasions, especially if you're a citrus lover, like me.

Ultimate Chocolate Fudge Cake

My Ultimate Chocolate Fudge Cake is everything you would imagine. A layer of moist, rich chocolaty sponge, topped with a decadent chocolate buttercream that is so heavenly smooth you'll be wanting to eat it with everything! A good, fail-safe chocolate cake recipe is something that I believe we all need to have in our arsenal. They're perfect for just about any occasion, and I've found this particular recipe to be my go-to for countless birthdays and dinner parties. You can't go too far wrong with a generous slice of chocolate fudge cake paired with some gloriously sweet fresh berries!

Preheat the oven to 355°F (180°C) and line an 8-inch (20-cm) loose-bottom cake pan with parchment paper.

To make the vegan buttermilk alternative, add the apple cider vinegar to the soy milk, stir and let it thicken for 5 minutes.

Next, in a large mixing bowl, combine the sugar and olive oil and, using a wooden spoon, mix until pale and fluffy. Add the buttermilk and yogurt, stirring to combine.

Sift the cocoa powder, flour, baking powder, baking soda and a generous pinch of salt into the bowl with the wet ingredients. Fold the ingredients and, using a wooden spoon, mix well until you're left with a smooth, chocolaty mixture.

Pour the batter into the cake pan and bake for 30 minutes.

Meanwhile, to make the frosting, start by beating the butter until pale and fluffy, using either a stand mixer or electric hand mixer. Gradually add the powdered sugar and cocoa powder and continue to mix until fully incorporated.

Gently melt the chocolate, then drizzle it into your frosting while gently whipping until fully incorporated.

(continued)

Yield: 10 Servings

CAKE

15 ml (1 tbsp) apple cider vinegar

120 ml (½ cup) soy milk

155 g (¾ cup) golden superfine or granulated sugar

100 ml (4 oz) olive oil or other neutral oil

70 g (3 oz) soy yogurt

30 g (¼ cup) high-quality cocoa powder

200 g (1⅝ cups) self-rising flour

1 tsp baking powder

⅓ tsp baking soda

Generous pinch of salt

FROSTING

150 g (¾ cup) vegan stick butter, at room temperature

125 g (⅝ cup) powdered sugar

20 g (¼ cup) high-quality cocoa powder

100 g (4 oz) roughly chopped vegan dark or milk chocolate

Ultimate Chocolate Fudge Cake (Continued)

Once your cake has cooled, spread the creamy chocolate frosting over the cake. Arrange the strawberries and raspberries around the edge of the cake to decorate along with the pomegranate seeds and chopped chocolate pieces.

TOPPINGS

100 g (⅔ cup) fresh strawberries, sliced

100 g (¾ cup) fresh raspberries, whole

100 g (4 oz) fresh pomegranate seeds

50 g (2 oz) roughly chopped vegan dark chocolate

Black Forest Layer Cake

Black Forest cake is an absolute classic dessert recipe that combines the rich flavor of chocolate sponge cake with a fresh and vibrant fruit compote and light whipped vanilla cream. Another feature of this cake is that it looks more impressive and complicated than it is, so it's definitely one to try if you're looking to impress! I love making this for special events or dinner parties, as it's always an impressive addition to the dessert table and, of course, tastes incredible!

Preheat your oven to 355°F (180°C) and line two 6½-inch (17-cm) loose-bottom cake pans with parchment paper.

To make the vegan buttermilk alternative, add the apple cider vinegar to the plant-based milk, stir and let thicken for 5 minutes.

Cream the olive oil and sugar together using a wooden spoon, then stir in the buttermilk and soy yogurt.

In a separate bowl, sift your self-rising flour, cocoa powder, baking powder and baking soda. Fold the dry ingredients into your wet mixture and continue until you have a smooth, chocolaty batter.

Pour the batter into the cake pans and bake for 30 to 32 minutes, then remove from the oven and allow to cool completely.

While the cakes are baking, make the cherry jam. Add your berries and cherries into a saucepan along with the water and maple syrup. Heat this over medium heat, then reduce to a simmer for 5 to 10 minutes. Once the berries have cooked down and released all the wonderful juices, remove them from the heat. Set these aside to cool and thicken in consistency.

(continued)

Yield: 8–12 Servings

CAKE

15 ml (1 tbsp) apple cider vinegar

200 ml (7 oz) plant-based milk (soy, almond or oat will work)

80 ml (3 oz) olive oil

180 g (⅞ cup) golden superfine or granulated sugar

80 g (⅓ cup) soy yogurt

260 g (2⅛ cups) self-rising flour

40 g (⅜ cup) cocoa powder

5 g (2 tsp) baking powder

⅓ tsp baking soda

JAM

100 g (¾ cup) fresh or frozen mixed berries

200 g (7 oz) pitted fresh cherries

100 ml (3 oz) water

30 ml (2 tbsp) maple syrup, plus more as desired

Black Forest Layer Cake (Continued)

To make the frosting, beat the butter until pale and fluffy using an electric hand whisk or stand mixer. Gradually whisk in the powdered sugar and vanilla until everything is well combined and super smooth.

Once your cakes have cooled, using a palette knife, spread a layer of frosting onto one of the cakes. Take a spoon and make a well in the frosting to create a dip in the center and raised outer edges. This will help to hold your jam filling. Add a few spoonfuls of cherry jam to the well and carefully place the second cake layer on top.

Spread an even layer of buttercream to cover the cake and, using a cake scraper, carefully smooth the buttercream. Use the remaining frosting to fill a piping bag fitted with a star nozzle and pipe swirls around the edge of the cake. Decorate with fresh cherries on top of the cake and chopped chocolate around the base.

FROSTING

250 g (1⅒ cups) vegan stick butter

300 g (1½ cups) powdered sugar

Dash of vanilla extract

TOPPINGS

150 g (1 cup) fresh cherries

80 g (3 oz) finely chopped vegan dark chocolate

Classic Vanilla Sponge Cake

I feel no baking book would be complete without an exceptional recipe for a classic vanilla cake. Such a simple, delicate flavor, yet it is absolutely perfect all by itself. This makes an excellent birthday cake, dinner party dessert or a mid-afternoon sweet treat!

Preheat your oven to 355°F (180°C) and line two 6½-inch (17-cm) loose-bottom cake pans with parchment paper.

To make the vegan buttermilk alternative, add the apple cider vinegar to the soy milk, stir and let thicken for 5 minutes.

Use a wooden spoon to cream the sugar and olive oil together for a minute to fully combine. Mix in the yogurt, vanilla and buttermilk and whisk until smooth.

Sift the self-rising flour, baking powder and baking soda into the same mixing bowl, then fold both the wet and dry ingredients together until smooth.

Pour the batter into the cake pans and bake for 30 to 32 minutes, until cooked through and lightly golden on top. Check to see if your cakes are ready by inserting a toothpick. If it comes out clean, the cakes are cooked through. Remove them from the oven and let cool on a wire rack.

Meanwhile, to make the vanilla buttercream frosting, beat the butter until pale and fluffy, which should take about 2 minutes. This can be done using an electric hand whisk or the whisk attachment on a stand mixer.

Continue to mix while gradually adding in the powdered sugar and then the vanilla. Once you're left with a smooth and creamy frosting, start assembling your cake by spreading a generous layer over one of the sponge cakes using a palette knife. Carefully place the second layer on top, then spread the remaining icing over the entire cake to cover. Use a palette knife and cake scraper to create a smooth and even finish.

Use the remaining icing to fill a piping bag fitted with a star-tip nozzle and pipe decorative swirls on top of the cake to finish. You can serve this as is or add some fresh berries around the edges to finish. I've used strawberries.

Yield: 8-10 Servings

CAKE
15 ml (1 tbsp) apple cider vinegar

120 ml (½ cup) soy milk

160 g (¾ cup) superfine or granulated sugar

80 ml (3 oz) olive oil or other light-colored neutral oil

75 g (⅓ cup) vanilla or plain soy yogurt

1 tsp vanilla bean paste or good-quality vanilla extract

250 g (2 cups) self-rising flour

5 g (2 tsp) baking powder

⅓ tsp baking soda

FROSTING
250 g (1¹⁄₁₀ cups) vegan stick butter, at room temperature

300 g (1½ cups) powdered sugar

½ tsp vanilla bean paste

TOPPING
150 g (1 cup) fresh strawberries, sliced

Vegan Victoria Sandwich

The Victoria sandwich is such a classic, quintessential British dessert. Composed of two layers of soft, light sponge cake and a glorious filling of sweet berry jam and luscious whipped cream, it's an iconic and perfect treat to accompany an afternoon tea. This has always been one of my absolute favorite cake flavors ever since I was a child, and this vegan adaptation is equally as delicious as the original!

Preheat your oven to 355°F (180°C) and line two 6½-inch (17-cm) loose-bottom cake pans with parchment paper.

To make the vegan buttermilk alternative, add the apple cider vinegar to the soy milk, stir and let thicken for 5 minutes.

In a large mixing bowl or stand mixer, add the olive oil and sugar, then using a wooden spoon, cream them together until pale and fluffy. This should take about 1 minute.

Pour in the buttermilk and vanilla and whisk. Sift in the self-rising flour, baking powder and baking soda. Add a pinch of salt and, using a wooden spoon, fold the wet and dry ingredients together until the mixture is smooth.

Divide the batter evenly between the cake pans and bake for 30 minutes, until lightly golden.

While the cake is baking, make the frosting. In a large mixing bowl or stand mixer, beat the butter until light and fluffy, then add the powdered sugar in increments while continuing to whisk. Once fully incorporated, your frosting should appear super thick and creamy!

To assemble the cake, start by adding a generous portion of buttercream to one of the layers and smooth this over. Top with the berry jam and layer with sliced strawberries. Carefully place the second layer on top and finish with the remaining frosting and strawberries, the raspberries and pomegranate seeds!

Yield: 8-10 Servings

CAKE

15 ml (1 tbsp) apple cider vinegar

220 ml (⅔ cup) soy milk

70 ml (3 oz) olive oil (light and mild)

175 g (¾ cup) superfine or granulated sugar

½ tsp vanilla bean paste

250 g (2 cups) self-rising flour

5 g (2 tsp) baking powder

⅓ tsp baking soda

Pinch of salt

FROSTING

250 g (1¹⁄₁₀ cups) vegan stick butter, room temperature

300 g (1½ cups) powdered sugar

ASSEMBLY

60 g (3 tbsp) strawberry or raspberry jam

200 g (1½ cups) fresh strawberries, sliced, plus more for topping

100 g (⅔ cup) fresh raspberries

60 g (2 oz) fresh pomegranate seeds

Red Velvet Cake

Red velvet cake is perfect for birthdays, a holiday dessert or any other special occasion. It's a super-moist sponge cake, with a gloriously vibrant color and subtle hint of cocoa flavor. This recipe uses freeze-dried beetroot powder as a natural food coloring, which, when combined with the rich cocoa powder, creates a stunning deep red hue. The sweet, yet bold flavors of this sponge pair beautifully with the delicate vanilla buttercream. You can also serve this with my classic vegan cream cheese frosting recipe (page 82) if you prefer.

Preheat your oven to 355°F (180°C) and line two 6½-inch (17-cm) loose-bottom cake pans with parchment paper.

To make the vegan buttermilk alternative, add the apple cider vinegar to the nondairy milk, stir and let thicken for 5 minutes.

In a large mixing bowl, use a wooden spoon to cream the olive oil and sugar together until fully combined. This should only take 1 to 2 minutes and the mixture will appear slightly pale and fluffy once ready.

Stir in the buttermilk and coconut yogurt to combine. Sift the flour, cocoa powder, baking powder and baking soda into the bowl and fold them into the wet mixture with a pinch of salt. Using a wooden spoon, stir these together until the batter is smooth.

Stir in the beetroot powder to create a beautifully red-colored batter. You can add a little extra powder if needed.

Divide your batter evenly between the two cake pans and pop these into the oven for 30 to 35 minutes. Once cooked, remove the cakes from the oven and transfer to a wire rack to cool completely.

(continued)

Yield 8-10 Servings

CAKE

15 ml (1 tbsp) apple cider vinegar

210 ml (7 oz) nondairy milk

80 ml (3 oz) olive oil

180 g (⅞ cup) golden superfine or granulated sugar

60 g (¼ cup) coconut yogurt

230 g (1⅞ cups) self-rising flour

20 g (¼ cup) cocoa powder

5 g (2 tsp) baking powder

⅓ tsp baking soda

Pinch of salt

2-4 g (1-2 tsp) freeze-dried beetroot powder or a few drops of vegan-friendly red food coloring

Red Velvet Cake (Continued)

While the cakes are cooling, make the frosting. Using an electric hand whisk or stand mixer on low to medium speed, beat the butter until pale and fluffy, then gradually incorporate the powdered sugar and vanilla.

Once you're left with a smooth and creamy frosting, it's time to assemble your cake. Spread a generous layer of the frosting over one of the cake layers and, using a palette knife, smooth it over. Carefully sandwich the second layer on top.

Using the remaining frosting, spread an even layer over the outside of the cake and use a cake scraper and palette knife to create a smooth, even finish. To decorate the cake, place the sliced strawberries and pomegranate seeds in the center.

Take the freeze-dried berries and press these around the base of the cake, as shown in the photo.

FROSTING

250 g (1$\frac{1}{10}$ cups) vegan stick butter, room temperature

300 g (1½ cups) powdered sugar

Dash of vanilla extract

TOPPINGS

200 g (1⅓ cups) fresh strawberries

50 g (2 oz) fresh pomegranate seeds

10 g (1/10 cup) freeze-dried berries (strawberries or raspberries would work)

Lemon Curd & Poppyseed Cake

When asked about my favorite dessert recipes or signature dishes, I will always opt for something fresh and citrus flavored. Anything involving lemon is always a winner for me, as I just adore the bright, tangy flavor it brings.

Lemon Curd & Poppyseed Cake combines that vibrant flavor with a hint of nuttiness and crunch from the poppyseeds. This teatime classic is perfect for a little mid-afternoon treat, as it's sweet yet still light enough to enjoy without feeling like you've over-indulged.

Preheat your oven to 355°F (180°C) and line two 6½-inch (17-cm) loose-bottom cake pans with parchment paper.

To make the vegan buttermilk alternative, add 1 tablespoon (15 ml) of the lemon juice to the soy milk, stir and let thicken for 5 minutes.

Add the lemon zest and sugar to a bowl and using your fingers, rub these together to infuse the sugar with citrus flavor. Use a wooden spoon to mix in the olive oil and vegan butter for 1 to 2 minutes, until pale and fluffy.

Pour in the buttermilk, remaining 2 tablespoons (30 ml) of lemon juice and vanilla then whisk together.

Sift the self-rising flour, baking powder and baking soda into the mixing bowl, then gently fold these together with the wet mixture to combine. Stir through the poppyseeds and divide the batter evenly between your cake pans.

Place these into the oven to bake for 30 to 35 minutes, until risen and lightly golden on top. Remove your cakes from the oven and transfer onto a wire rack to cool thoroughly.

(continued)

Yield: 8-10 Servings

CAKE

45 ml (3 tbsp) lemon juice, divided

200 ml (7 oz) soy milk

Zest from 2 lemons

180 g (⅞ cup) superfine or granulated sugar

40 ml (3 tbsp) olive oil

40 g (⅛ cup) vegan stick butter

½ tsp vanilla extract

240 g (1⅞ cups) self-rising flour

5 g (2 tsp) baking powder

⅓ tsp baking soda

2 tbsp poppyseeds

Lemon Curd & Poppyseed Cake (Continued)

In the meantime, make the passion fruit and lemon curd. In a saucepan, combine the lemon juice, passion fruit, nondairy milk, sugar and lemon zest. Gently heat these together over medium heat to allow the sugar to dissolve.

Whisk in the corn starch, bring to a boil, then reduce to a simmer and allow the curd to thicken, 5 to 10 minutes. Transfer this to a bowl and place in the fridge to cool and thicken in consistency.

To make the buttercream frosting, start by beating the butter until pale and fluffy, which should take about 2 minutes. This can either be done using an electric hand mixer or stand mix.

Incorporate the sugar and lemon zest by gradually adding these in while mixing. Repeat this until you're left with a smooth and creamy buttercream.

To assemble the cake, spread a layer of frosting onto one of your sponge cakes and using a spoon, create a small well in the center. Add a few tablespoons of the homemade curd in the center and carefully place the second sponge cake layer on top of this.

Take the remaining frosting and spread this over the outside of the entire cake using a palette knife. Use a cake scraper to help smooth this buttercream coating and create an even finish.

For decorations, arrange the lemon slices and flowers, if using, in the center of the cake and drizzle with some extra passionfruit and lemon curd.

PASSION FRUIT & LEMON CURD

Juice from 2 lemons

Filling from 2 fresh passion fruit

100 ml (3 oz) nondairy milk

100 g (½ cup) superfine or granulated sugar

Zest from 2 lemons

9 g (3 tsp) corn starch

FROSTING

250 g (1¹⁄₁₀ cups) vegan stick butter, at room temperature

300 g (1½ cups) powdered sugar

Zest from 2 lemons

TOPPINGS

Lemon slices

Edible flowers (optional)

Passionfruit and lemon curd

Coffee & Walnut Cake

This recipe for a classic Coffee & Walnut Cake is going to become your new favorite go-to for satisfying those afternoon tea and cake cravings. Layers of soft, coffee-infused sponge cake are sandwiched together with one of the most heavenly frosting recipes that you're ever going to experience!

Preheat your oven to 355°F (180°C) and line two 6½-inch (17-cm) loose-bottom cake pans with parchment paper.

To make the vegan buttermilk alternative, add the apple cider vinegar to the almond milk, stir and let thicken for 5 minutes.

In a large mixing bowl, use a wooden spoon to cream the olive oil, superfine sugar and light brown sugar together.

Once combined, whisk in the buttermilk and strong-brewed espresso.

Sift the flour, baking powder and baking soda and fold these into the wet ingredients. Once your batter is completely smooth, stir in the chopped walnuts and divide the mixture evenly between your cake pans.

Bake for 30 minutes, until well risen and golden on top. Remove from the oven and allow to cool on a wire rack.

To make the coffee frosting, beat the butter until pale and fluffy, then gradually incorporate the powdered sugar. Mix the instant espresso, to taste, with 2 teaspoons (10 ml) of water, and add the mixture to the frosting. I love coffee, so I always opt for 2 teaspoons (4 g) of instant espresso, but this is totally up to you!

Once your cakes have cooled, spread a generous layer of the frosting over one of the cakes and smooth it all around with a palette knife. Place the second cake layer on top and cover it with the remaining buttercream, reserving some for decorating the cake.

To decorate your cake, heat the Biscoff spread in the microwave for 10 to 20 seconds until melted. Spread it over the top of the cake, allowing it to drip over the edges. Garnish with some buttercream swirls and top each one with a coffee bean.

Yield: 10–12 Servings

CAKE

15 ml (1 tbsp) apple cider vinegar

150 ml (5 oz) almond milk

90 ml (6 tbsp) olive oil

160 g (¾ cup) golden superfine or granulated sugar

45 g (¼ cup) light brown sugar

60 ml (2 oz) strong-brewed espresso

250 g (2 cups) self-rising flour

5 g (2 tsp) baking powder

⅓ tsp baking soda

80 g (⅔ cup) chopped walnuts

FROSTING

200 g (⅞ cup) vegan stick butter, room temperature

270 g (2 cups) powdered sugar

2–4 g (1–2 tsp) instant espresso

TOPPING

50 grams (3 heaped tbsp) Lotus Biscoff® spread

Coffee beans

Tres Leches Cake

Although it is a classic dessert, Tres Leches Cake isn't just your average sheet cake! Tres leches translates as "three milks," which, when combined, creates a lusciously sweet and creamy mixture to infuse into a fluffy vanilla sponge cake. I've given this recipe a slight twist with the addition of desiccated coconut and coconut milk for an additional hint of delicate, fragrant flavor.

Preheat your oven to 355°F (180°C) and line a 9-inch (23-cm) baking pan (I usually use a brownie pan for this) with parchment paper.

To make the vegan buttermilk alternative, add the apple cider vinegar to the soy milk, stir and let thicken for 5 minutes.

In a large mixing bowl, add the olive oil and sugar and beat together using a wooden spoon until well combined. Pour in the buttermilk and vanilla, then mix these together until thoroughly incorporated.

Sift in the self-rising flour, baking powder and baking soda and gently fold into the wet mixture until fully combined. Pour in the desiccated coconut and stir it into the batter.

Pour the batter into your lined baking pan and bake for 30 minutes.

Meanwhile, whisk together the vegan heavy cream, condensed milk and coconut milk.

Once your cake is ready, remove it from the oven and use a fork to pierce all over the cake. Pour the mixture of milks over the cake and allow it to soak into the sponge. Cover the cake and leave it to chill in the fridge for 2 to 3 hours.

You can serve the cake as it is or whip up some vegan whipping cream and layer this over the top, and add some fresh berries and pomegranate seeds to finish!

Yield: 8 Servings

CAKE

15 ml (1 tbsp) apple cider vinegar

250 ml (8 oz) soy milk

100 ml (4 oz) olive oil

200 g (1 cup) superfine or granulated sugar

Dash of vanilla extract

230 g (1⅞ cups) self-rising flour

5 g (2 tsp) baking powder

⅓ tsp baking soda

30 g (⅓ cup) desiccated coconut

100 ml (½ cup) vegan heavy cream

230 ml (1 cup) vegan condensed milk

125 ml (½ cup) coconut milk

TOPPING

250 ml (1 cup) vegan whipping cream

150 g (¾ cup) fresh strawberries

100 g (⅔ cup) fresh raspberries

100 g (3.5 oz) fresh pomegranate seeds

The Best Vegan Coconut Cake

This is making somewhat of a bold statement, but I do believe that this is the best vegan coconut cake that I've had the pleasure of eating! I'm obsessed with anything coconut flavored, so the recipe is a favorite of mine!

Preheat the oven to 355°F (180°C) and line two 6½-inch (17-cm) loose-bottom cake pans with parchment paper.

To make the vegan buttermilk alternative, add the apple cider vinegar to the nondairy milk, stir and let thicken for 5 minutes.

In a large mixing bowl, cream the olive oil and sugar together until slightly pale and fluffy. Pour in the buttermilk and vanilla and mix well using a wooden spoon.

Sift in the self-rising flour, baking powder and baking soda and using a wooden spoon, fold these into the wet ingredients until fully combined. Add a pinch of salt and the desiccated coconut and stir thoroughly.

Divide the batter between both the lined cake pans and bake for 30 to 35 minutes, until lightly golden and risen. Remove the cakes from the oven and allow them to cool completely.

In the meantime, you can prepare the delicious frosting. Add the butter to a stand mixer or use an electric hand whisk. Beat until gloriously pale and fluffy, then gradually add the powdered sugar while continuing to mix.

When your frosting is fully mixed and perfectly smooth, stir in the desiccated coconut.

To assemble the cake, spread a generous layer of the vegan buttercream on one of the cake layers using a palette knife and place the second cake on top. Use the remaining buttercream and use a palette knife to apply a thin, even layer of buttercream over the entire cake. Then, take a cake scraper and use this to smooth and even out the frosting.

Carefully press the coconut against the frosted cake to coat it entirely. Add the berries and pomegranate seeds to garnish and finish with some mint leaves for freshness.

Yield: 8-10 Servings

CAKE
15 ml (1 tbsp) apple cider vinegar

200 ml (7 oz) nondairy milk

80 ml (3 oz) olive oil

180 g (⅞ cup) sugar

½ tsp vanilla bean paste

250 g (2 cups) self-rising flour

5 g (2 tsp) baking powder

¼ tsp baking soda

Pinch of salt

40 g (½ cup) desiccated coconut

FROSTING
250 g (1¹⁄₁₀ cups) vegan stick butter, room temperature

300 g (1½ cups) powdered sugar

30 g (⅓ cup) desiccated coconut

TOPPINGS
200 g (2 cups) desiccated coconut

250 g (1 cup) fresh mixed berries of choice

100 g (3.5 oz) fresh pomegranate seeds

Fresh mint leaves

Zesty Madeira Cake

Madeira cake was a family favorite in my household and for good reason! Its soft, buttery texture is the perfect pairing for an afternoon cup of tea, and it is so quick and simple to make! Despite being completely dairy free and plant based, this cake still has an incredibly moist, fluffy texture. Without butter! This traditionally classic cake is flavored with subtle hints of orange, lemon and vanilla, making it an idyllic sweet snack for all occasions! I love serving this at summer dinner parties and afternoon tea, accompanied with fresh seasonal fruit and whipped coconut cream. It's simply divine!

Preheat your oven to 355°F (180°C) and line an 8-inch (20-cm) loose-bottom cake pan with parchment paper.

To make the vegan buttermilk alternative, add the apple cider vinegar to the soy milk, stir and let thicken for 5 minutes.

Add the sugar and olive oil to a large mixing bowl, then cream these together using a wooden spoon. After 1 to 2 minutes, when the mixture is slightly pale and fluffy, stir in the buttermilk until fully combined.

Sift the self-rising flour, baking powder and baking soda and add these into your mixing bowl along with the salt, lemon zest, orange zest and vanilla. Fold everything together carefully until you're left with a completely lump-free batter.

Pour the batter into your lined cake pan and bake for 40 to 45 minutes. Check to see if your cakes are ready by inserting a toothpick. If it comes out clean, the cakes are cooked through.

Allow your cake to cool for 5 minutes in the pan, then transfer to a wire rack to cool completely.

To garnish, top with some nondairy whipped cream, your favorite seasonal fruits and fresh mint leaves!

Yield: 8-10 Servings

CAKE

15 ml (1 tbsp) apple cider vinegar

220 ml (⅔ cup) soy milk

170 g (¾ cups) superfine or granulated sugar

75 ml (3 oz) olive oil

240 g (1⅞ cups) self-rising flour

5 g (2 tsp) baking powder

½ tsp baking soda

Pinch of salt

Zest from 1 lemon

Zest from 1 orange

1 tsp vanilla bean paste

TOPPINGS

Nondairy whipped cream

200 g (7 oz) fresh seasonal fruit

Fresh mint leaves

Layer Cakes

As I found my baking niche and perfected my craft, I really developed a passion for baking layer cakes. I love the process of being able to bring flavors and ingredients that I love into the form of a magnificent, tiered cake. A layer cake is simply the epitome of a decadent dessert and this selection of recipes is here to show you just how incredible and easy creating plant-based varieties can be. There are layers of soft, moist sponge cakes with the most divine, creamy vegan frostings and a heaping of glorious toppings and drizzles! By switching certain ingredients for plant-based alternatives, it couldn't be simpler to re-create your most loved bakes!

I find a lot of my inspiration for flavors in my favorite everyday desserts and sweet treats. Whether that be popular dessert flavor combinations, biscuits, ice-cream flavors . . . anything works really, and the possibilities are endless! With that being said, I can't help but urge you to try my Lotus Biscoff® Layer Cake (page 41), as this is simply heavenly! I'm a huge cookie-butter spread lover, so for me, this cake is pure perfection! It's suitable for all seasons and occasions, and most of the ingredients are items that I already have in my kitchen cupboards. Just think fluffy, biscuit-infused sponge cake with a sweet buttercream and notes of caramel all drizzled in melted cookie-butter spread.

I've included a selection of my most-loved layer cake recipes, ranging from simple to more intricate bakes. There's a variety of different flavor combinations and frostings, all of which are, of course, completely plant based! Not only do these cakes taste exceptionally delicious, but I can also guarantee that they will be the star of your table spread!

Lotus Biscoff® Layer Cake

The Lotus Biscoff® Layer Cake is a real crowd-pleasing showstopper that I can guarantee will be a treat on any occasion. Layers of fluffy vanilla Biscoff sponge cake, sandwiched together with a whipped Biscoff frosting and finished with a generous buttercream layer and melted Biscoff drizzle! The rich caramel biscuit notes create an incredible flavor contrast with the sweet, airy buttercream frosting. Everything about this cake will leave you drooling; it's absolute cookie-butter heaven!

Preheat the oven to 355°F (180°C) and line your 6½-inch (17-cm) loose-bottom cake pans with parchment paper.

To make the vegan buttermilk alternative, add the apple cider vinegar to the soy milk, stir and let thicken for 5 minutes.

In a large mixing bowl, combine the sugar and olive oil and cream together until pale and fluffy.

Stir in the buttermilk and vanilla. Sift in the flour, baking powder and baking soda. Gently fold these into the wet mixture along with a pinch of salt and mix until smooth.

Place the biscuits into a ziplock bag and crush using a rolling pin. Pour these into the cake batter and stir through to evenly distribute.

Transfer the mixture to your cake pans and bake for 30 to 35 minutes. Check to see if your cakes are ready by inserting a toothpick. If it comes out clean, the cakes are cooked through.

Once ready, remove the cakes from the oven and transfer onto a wire rack to cool.

Yield: 8–10 Servings

CAKE

15 ml (1 tbsp) apple cider vinegar

180 ml (6 oz) soy milk

180 g (⅞ cup) golden superfine or granulated sugar

80 ml (3 oz) olive oil

½ tsp vanilla bean paste

250 g (2 cups) self-rising flour

5 g (2 tsp) baking powder

⅓ tsp baking soda

Pinch of salt

80 g (3 oz) Lotus Biscoff® biscuits

(continued)

Lotus Biscoff® Layer Cake (Continued)

Whip up the frosting by beating the butter until pale and fluffy, which should take 5 minutes. I like to use an electric hand whisk or stand mixer.

Gradually add the powdered sugar and continue to mix until all the sugar has been incorporated. You can then fold in your creamy Biscoff spread to finish.

To assemble, spread a layer of the frosting onto one of the sponge cakes and make a small well in the center using the back of a spoon. This helps to avoid the filling spilling over the sides of the cake. Fill this with your cookie spread and place the second sponge on top.

Coat the entire cake in the delicious frosting and use a cake scraper and palette knife to achieve a smooth finish. Refrigerate the frosted cake for 5 to 10 minutes (doing so will help avoid your Biscoff drizzle from melting the frosting).

Gently melt the Biscoff spread and drizzle this around the edges of the cake, creating a drip effect. To melt the spread quickly, you can use a microwave, checking at 15-second intervals.

Add the remaining frosting to a piping bag, fitted with a star-tip nozzle, and pipe swirls all around the edge of your cake. Garnish with Lotus Biscoff biscuits and serve.

FROSTING

250 g (1¹⁄₁₀ cups) vegan stick butter, room temperature

300 g (1½ cups) powdered sugar

45 g (3 tbsp) Lotus Biscoff® spread

FILLING

45 g (3 tbsp) Lotus Biscoff spread

TOPPINGS

45 g (3 tbsp) Lotus Biscoff spread, for drizzling

Lotus Biscoff biscuits, as desired

The Best Salted Caramel Cake

I've always been a sucker for the sweet and salty flavor combination and feel like the addition of salt really enhances the sweetness in dessert recipes. If you're a salted caramel lover, then this cake is going to be right up your alley. There's a deliciously sweet sponge cake, paired with a creamy caramel frosting and rich, homemade vegan caramel sauce. This caramel sauce is also delightfully simple to make from scratch, which means you can now enjoy dairy-free salted caramel whenever you fancy. It also includes a secret ingredient (almond butter!), which adds an extra dimension of flavor to the caramel sauce with its rich nutty notes!

Preheat the oven to 355°F (180°C) and line 6½-inch (17-cm) loose-bottom cake pans with parchment paper.

To make the vegan buttermilk alternative, add the apple cider vinegar to the soy milk, stir and let thicken for 5 minutes.

Add the sugar and olive oil to a large mixing bowl and cream them together using a wooden spoon or electric hand whisk. Pour in the buttermilk and yogurt and stir to combine.

For the dry ingredients, sift the flour, baking powder and baking soda. Fold these into the wet ingredients and add a pinch of salt.

Pour the batter into your cake pans and bake for 30 minutes, then remove from the oven and transfer to a wire rack.

While the cakes cool, you can make the vegan caramel and frosting.

To make the vegan caramel, add the sugar and water to a small saucepan over medium-high heat. Swirl the pan around until the sugar dissolves. Do not mix at this stage because doing so could cause the sugar to stick and burn. Allow the mixture to bubble for a few minutes, then reduce to a simmer.

When the sugar has thickened to form a simple syrup, whisk in the almond butter, salt and vegan butter.

(continued)

Yield 8–10 Servings

CAKE

15 ml (1 tbsp) apple cider vinegar

150 ml (5 oz) soy milk

185 g (⅞ cup) golden superfine or granulated sugar

85 ml (3 oz) olive oil

80 g (⅓ cup) soy or coconut yogurt

250 g (2 cups) self-rising flour

5 g (2 tsp) baking powder

⅓ tsp baking soda

Pinch of sea salt

VEGAN SALTED CARAMEL

140 g (⅔ cup) superfine or granulated sugar

60 ml (2 oz) water

14 g (1 heaping tbsp) smooth almond butter

Generous pinch of sea salt

28 g (2 tbsp) vegan stick butter

The Best Salted Caramel Cake (Continued)

Pour in the milk and bring to a boil once more. When your caramel is bubbling and golden in color, remove from the heat while continuing to whisk. Allow the mixture to cool and thicken for 30 minutes, which should leave you with a gorgeous caramel consistency.

To make the frosting, add the butter to a large mixing bowl and, using an electric hand whisk, beat until pale and fluffy. Gradually incorporate the powdered sugar while whisking, then add the caramel sauce.

To assemble, place one layer of the cake onto your serving plate and spread over an even layer of buttercream. Make a slight well in the middle of the layer and build up around the sides, which will help to hold the caramel filling.

Add a few tablespoons (45 ml) of your homemade salted caramel, then place the second cake layer on top.

Coat the entire cake in a thick buttercream layer, then use a cake scraper and spatula to smooth the surface and create an even coating.

Take a tablespoon (15 ml) of vegan caramel at a time and drizzle it around the edges of your cake, allowing it to drip over the sides.

Transfer the remaining frosting to a piping bag with a star nozzle and carefully pipe around the edges of the cake, as shown in the photo.

I love to add extra caramel sauce to the center and top with fresh berries!

50 ml (¼ cup) nondairy milk

FROSTING

250 g (1¹⁄₁₀ cups) vegan stick butter

300 g (1½ cups) powdered sugar

30 ml (2 tbsp) homemade vegan salted caramel (see page 43)

½ tsp vanilla bean paste

TOPPINGS

Extra caramel sauce, as desired

Blackberries or other fresh berries of choice

Tiramisu Layer Cake

For me, this Tiramisu Layer Cake really is the perfect hybrid between a showstopping special occasion cake and something simple enough to enjoy as an everyday dessert. I'm a huge coffee lover, so a slice of this with a cup of coffee after lunch is my idea of heaven! The sponge cake is incredibly moist, infused with rich caramel notes of espresso and vanilla. This is then topped with a delicious vanilla coffee buttercream frosting, to which you can also add further indulgence by stirring in a little melted white chocolate!

Preheat your oven to 355°F (180°C) and line two 6½-inch (17-cm) loose-bottom cake pans with parchment paper.

To make the vegan buttermilk alternative, add the apple cider vinegar to the oat milk, stir and let thicken for 5 minutes.

In a bowl, cream together the olive oil and sugar. Add the buttermilk, espresso and vanilla and stir to combine.

Sift the flour, baking powder, baking soda and a pinch of salt and fold them into the wet ingredients. Once smooth, divide the batter between the cake pans and bake for 30 minutes.

(continued)

Yield: 8-10 Servings

CAKE

15 ml (1 tbsp) apple cider vinegar

140 ml (½ cup) oat milk

80 ml (3 oz) olive oil

180 g (⅞ cup) golden superfine or granulated sugar

60 ml (2 oz) strong-brewed espresso

1 tsp vanilla bean paste

240 g (1⅞ cups) self-rising flour

5 g (2 tsp) baking powder

⅓ tsp baking soda

Pinch of salt

Tiramisu Layer Cake (Continued)

While the cakes are cooling, make the frosting. Beat the butter and vegan cream cheese together until pale and fluffy, then gradually whisk in the powdered sugar, coffee mixture and vanilla. Once your buttercream is perfectly smooth, you can then fold in the melted white chocolate, if using.

To make the coffee syrup, mix the espresso and maple syrup.

Use a fork to pierce holes all over the surface of each cake, then pour the coffee syrup over and allow it to soak through.

Next, spread a generous helping of buttercream onto one of your cooled sponges and place the second on top. Using a cake scraper and spatula to ensure an even finish, smooth over the entire cake with the frosting. Transfer the remaining buttercream into a piping bag with a French star nozzle and pipe small swirls to decorate.

I love to finish with a dusting of cinnamon sugar and some fresh berries!

FROSTING

250 g (1¹⁄₁₀ cups) vegan stick butter, room temperature

75 g (⅓ cup) vegan cream cheese

310 g (1⅓ cup) powdered sugar

2–4 g (1–2 tsp) instant coffee mixed with 5 ml (2 tsp) water

1 tsp vanilla bean paste

50 g (2 oz) vegan white chocolate, chopped and melted (optional)

COFFEE SYRUP

80 ml (2 oz) fresh espresso

15–30 ml (1–2 tbsp) maple syrup

TOPPINGS

Cinnamon sugar

Blueberries or other fresh fruit

Lemon Curd & Coconut Cake

My Lemon Curd & Coconut Cake is the ultimate lemon cake. Whether you're a lemon-dessert obsessive like me or not, you're simply going to love this cake. The contrast between the sharp vegan lemon curd and light, fragrant coconut is truly mouthwatering and pairs perfectly with this soft and fluffy sponge cake. I feel like homemade lemon curd also needs a special mention of its own, as it's honestly so simple, yet tastes like a citrus flavor explosion! It's a great staple recipe to have on hand for adding to dessert and breakfast spreads.

Preheat your oven to 355°F (180°C) and line three 6½-inch (17-cm) loose-bottom cake pans with parchment paper.

To make the vegan buttermilk alternative, add the lemon juice to the nondairy milk, stir and let thicken for 5 minutes.

Combine the sugar and olive oil in a large mixing bowl and beat together using a wooden spoon. Add the buttermilk and vanilla and whisk thoroughly.

Sift the self-rising flour, baking powder and baking soda. Fold these into your wet ingredients, adding in the desiccated coconut and lemon zest. Once everything is fully combined and you're left with a nice, smooth mixture, divide it evenly among the three cake pans and bake for 30 minutes.

While the cakes are baking, make the vegan lemon curd. In a medium saucepan, combine the lemon juice, zest, nondairy milk and sugar. Gently heat these over a medium heat to allow the sugar to dissolve. Whisk in the corn starch and bring to a boil. Reduce to a simmer and continue to mix as your curd thickens. Remove from the heat and allow it to cool for 30 minutes.

Once your cakes have risen and appear golden, remove them from the oven and allow them to cool completely.

(continued)

Yield: 8-10 Servings

CAKE

15 ml (1 tbsp) lemon juice

200 ml (7 oz) nondairy milk

180 g (⅞ cup) superfine or granulated sugar

90 ml (6 tbsp) olive oil

1 tsp vanilla extract

240 g (1⅞ cups) self-rising flour

7 g (1½ tsp) baking powder

⅓ tsp baking soda

50 g (½ cup) desiccated coconut

Zest from 2 lemons

LEMON CURD

Juice from 2 lemons

Zest from 2 lemons

100 ml (3 oz) nondairy milk

100 g (½ cup) superfine or granulated sugar

9 g (3 tsp) corn starch

Lemon Curd & Coconut Cake (Continued)

To make the lemon and coconut frosting, start by beating the butter until pale and fluffy. This should take about 5 minutes and you can either use an electric hand whisk or a stand mixer.

Gradually incorporate the powdered sugar while mixing and continue until fully combined and super creamy. Fold in the lemon zest and vanilla.

Melt the white chocolate in a small saucepan over low heat and gently whip this into your frosting along with the coconut milk.

To assemble your cake, spread an even layer of frosting over one of the layers, making a slight well in the center. Add a few spoonfuls of lemon curd and sandwich a second sponge layer on top.

Repeat this process with the final layer, then use the remaining frosting to add a generous whipped topping.

I love to top this cake with fresh fruit, especially berries. However, you can also add some lemon slices or white chocolate shavings!

FROSTING

250 g (1¹⁄₁₀ cups) vegan stick butter, room temperature

300 g (1½ cups) powdered sugar

Zest from 1 lemon

Dash of vanilla extract

60 g (2 oz) vegan white chocolate, chopped

45 ml (3 tbsp) canned coconut milk or cream

TOPPING

Fresh fruit, like berries or lemon slices

White chocolate (optional)

Chocolate Orange Layer Cake

There's no doubt about it, chocolate and orange are an iconic flavor combination. I don't know what exactly it is about it, but the flavors just seem to work together in such harmony. The dark, rich notes of cocoa and sweet, slightly sour citrus flavors are a perfect contrast. My Chocolate Orange Layer Cake is mouthwateringly moist, has a rich chocolate flavor and the most incredibly creamy ganache frosting. Each bite is a complete explosion of indulgence—you honestly won't believe this dessert is vegan!

Preheat your oven to 355°F (180°C) and line two 6-inch (15-cm) loose-bottom cake pans with parchment paper.

To make the vegan buttermilk alternative, add the lemon juice to the oat milk, stir and let thicken for 5 minutes.

In a large mixing bowl, beat the olive oil and sugar until pale and fluffy.

Pour in the buttermilk, vanilla and orange zest, then stir to combine. Sift the cocoa powder, flour, baking powder and baking soda.

Fold the wet and dry ingredients together so that you're left with a smooth, creamy batter. Transfer this into your cake pans and bake for 30 to 35 minutes.

Once cooked through, remove and allow to cool completely.

To make the ganache filling, set up a heatproof bowl over a saucepan of gently boiling water and add the chocolate. Allow this to melt, then remove from the heat and whisk in the coconut milk. Add the maple syrup, if using. Allow the mixture to cool and thicken.

(continued)

Yield: 10 Servings

CAKE

15 ml (1 tbsp) lemon juice

200 ml (7 oz) oat milk

90 ml (3 oz) olive oil

200 g (1 cup) superfine or granulated sugar

½ tsp vanilla bean paste

Zest from 1½ oranges

40 g (⅜ cup) high-quality cocoa powder

200 g (1⅝ cups) self-rising flour

9 g (2 tsp) baking powder

⅓ tsp baking soda

GANACHE FILLING

100 g (4 oz) vegan dark orange chocolate, chopped

70 ml (¼ cup) canned full-fat coconut milk

Maple or agave syrup (optional)

Chocolate Orange Layer Cake (Continued)

For the ganache frosting, beat the butter until pale and fluffy using either an electric hand whisk or stand mixer. Gradually whisk in the powdered sugar and cocoa powder until fully combined. Pour in the coconut milk and melted chocolate and continue whisking to form a velvety smooth texture.

To assemble, spread a layer of frosting onto one of your cakes using a palette knife. With the back of a spoon, make a small well in the center to hold the filling and prevent any overspill. Add about 45 milliliters (3 tablespoons) of your ganache filling, reserving the remaining ganache for another recipe, then place the second cake layer on top.

Cover the entire cake in your creamy frosting and use a cake scraper to smooth the sides and create an even finish.

Transfer the remaining frosting into a piping bag and pipe decorative swirls on top. Garnish with slices of orange and some chopped dark chocolate.

GANACHE FROSTING

230 g (1 cup) vegan stick butter, room temperature

290 g (1½ cups) powdered sugar

20 g (¼ cup) high-quality cocoa powder

50 ml (¼ cup) canned coconut milk

50 g (2 oz) melted vegan dark chocolate

TOPPINGS

Orange slices

60 g (2 oz) vegan dark chocolate, chopped into shards

Mint Chocolate-Chip Layer Cake

For me, mint and chocolate is such a great combination and one that I've always loved! I distinctly remember mint chocolate chip being the only ice-cream flavor, aside from vanilla, that I would repeatedly order from the seaside ice-cream stalls. So this flavor combination is quite nostalgic for me. This cake consists of layers of peppermint-flavored sponge cake, sandwiched together with a creamy chocolate ganache and finished with a mint-chocolate buttercream coating. This is the ideal cake for any mint fan, and the frosting alone is something you'll be wanting to make time and time again!

Preheat your oven to 355°F (180°C) and line two 6½-inch (17-cm) loose-bottom cake pans with parchment paper.

To make the vegan buttermilk alternative, add the apple cider vinegar to the soy milk, stir and let thicken for 5 minutes.

Place the sugar and olive oil into a mixing bowl and cream together until pale and fluffy.

Add the sifted flour, baking powder, baking soda, vanilla and peppermint extract. Fold the wet and dry ingredients together to fully combine, then stir in the chocolate chips.

Pour the mixture into the cake pans and bake for 30 minutes, then allow to cool on a wire rack.

Meanwhile, make the frosting. Use an electric hand whisk or stand mixer on low to medium speed to cream the butter until pale and fluffy. Gradually add the powdered sugar and continue to mix until it is fully incorporated and your frosting is super creamy. Mix in the peppermint extract and a touch of food coloring, then fold through the chopped dark chocolate for that speckled effect.

(continued)

Yield: 8-10 Servings

CAKE

15 ml (1 tbsp) apple cider vinegar

200 ml (7 oz) soy milk

200 g (1 cup) superfine or granulated sugar

80 ml (3 oz) olive oil

240 g (1⅞ cups) self-rising flour, sifted

5 g (2 tsp) baking powder

⅓ tsp baking soda

½ tsp vanilla paste

½–1 tsp peppermint extract

60 g (2 oz) vegan dark chocolate chips

FROSTING

250 g (1¹⁄₁₀ cups) vegan stick butter

300 g (1½ cups) powdered sugar

Dash of peppermint extract

Dash of vegan green food coloring

50 g (2 oz) chopped dark chocolate

Mint Chocolate-Chip Layer Cake (Continued)

For the ganache filling, melt the chocolate and cream together in a heatproof bowl placed over a saucepan of gently boiling water, then remove it from the heat and let it cool and thicken.

To assemble the cake, spread an even coating of buttercream over one of your sponges and create a small well in the center using the back of a spoon. This will prevent the filling spilling over the sides of the cake. Fill the well with the chocolate ganache.

Place the second cake layer on top, then coat your cake in a thick layer of peppermint buttercream. Gently smooth the frosting using a cake scraper to achieve a beautifully even finish. Place the cake in the fridge for 5 to 10 minutes to set the buttercream.

To finish, melt the chocolate and coconut oil together over low heat, then carefully drizzle this around the edges of your cake. I use any remaining frosting to pipe some extra swirls and then finish with fresh mint leaves.

GANACHE FILLING

100 g (4 oz) vegan milk chocolate

125 ml (4 oz) vegan whipping cream

TOPPINGS

80 g (3 oz) vegan dark chocolate, chopped

1 tsp coconut oil

Fresh mint leaves

Cookies & Cream Layer Cake

If you're an Oreo® fan, then this is undoubtedly the cake for you! Two layers of fluffy vanilla sponge cake complete with tiny bites of Oreo cookies throughout. This is the perfect balance between sweet notes of vanilla and rich indulgent chocolate, so you can enjoy the best of both worlds!

Preheat your oven to 355°F (180°C). Line two 6-inch (15-cm) cake pans with parchment paper.

To make the vegan buttermilk alternative, add the apple cider vinegar to the almond milk, stir and let thicken for 5 minutes.

Place the butter, olive oil and sugar in a large mixing bowl and use a wooden spoon to cream these together. Once your mixture is pale and fluffy, whisk in the buttermilk and vanilla.

Sift the flour, baking powder and baking soda. Fold these into the wet ingredients with a pinch of salt.

Pop the cookies into a freezer bag and crush them into crumbs using a rolling pin. Stir the crumbs into the cake batter and divide the batter evenly between the two cake pans.

Bake for 30 minutes, then remove from the oven and let them cool in the pan for 10 minutes, then transfer onto a wire rack.

To make the cookies and cream frosting, beat the butter in a stand or hand mixer at medium speed until pale and fluffy.

Add the powdered sugar gradually while continuously mixing to create a smooth, creamy frosting. Crush the cookies using the same technique as before, then fold these into the buttercream.

Once the cakes have cooled, spread some of the frosting over one layer and carefully place the second on top. Layer the remaining frosting, reserving some for decorating, all over the cake and use a cake scraper and spatula to smooth the sides.

Place your frosted cake into the fridge for 5 to 10 minutes to prevent the frosting from melting. For the drip effect, melt the chocolate and coconut oil together. Pour these over the top of the cake and use a small offset spatula to spread this toward the edges, allowing it to run over the sides, then top with swirls of buttercream and more Oreo cookies!

Yield: 8–10 Servings

CAKE

15 ml (1 tbsp) apple cider vinegar

160 ml (5 oz) almond milk

35 g (⅛ cup) vegan butter

35 ml (4 oz) olive oil

155 g (¾ cup) superfine or granulated sugar

½ tsp vanilla bean paste

240 g (1⅞ cups) self-rising flour

9 g (2 tsp) baking powder

⅓ tsp baking soda

Pinch of salt

8 Oreo® cookies

FROSTING

250 g (1¹¹⁄₁₀ cups) vegan stick butter, room temperature

300 g (1½ cups) powdered sugar

5 Oreo cookies

TOPPINGS

80 g (3 oz) vegan dark chocolate

Extra Oreo cookies

S'mores Layer Cake

This layer cake combines elements of a favorite summertime treat to create an incredibly indulgent chocolate and marshmallow heaven. Plus, this version doesn't require a campfire; in fact, it's actually far simpler to make than you might think. The base of the cake is a perfectly moist chocolate, biscuity sponge cake. The two layers are sandwiched together with a creamy vanilla frosting and topped with glorious lashings of melted dark chocolate and a homemade marshmallow frosting. This frosting is a total game changer and really adds that showstopping effect to this cake!

Preheat the oven to 355°F (180°C) and line two 6½-inch (17-cm) cake pans with parchment paper.

To make the vegan buttermilk alternative, add the lemon juice to the soy milk, stir and let thicken for 5 minutes.

In a mixing bowl, beat the sugar and olive oil until well mixed. Pour in the canned coconut milk, buttermilk and vanilla and whisk together.

Sift the cocoa powder, self-rising flour, baking powder and baking soda and fold these into the wet mixture with the cinnamon, mixed spice and a pinch of salt.

Pop your biscuits into a freezer bag and crush with a rolling pin. Stir these through your batter and transfer to the cake pans. Bake the cakes for 30 minutes. Check to see if your cakes are ready by inserting a toothpick. If it comes out clean, the cakes are cooked through.

(continued)

Yield: 8–10 Servings

CAKE

15 ml (1 tbsp) lemon juice

110 ml (4 oz) soy milk

180 g (⅞ cup) superfine or granulated sugar

80 ml (3 oz) olive oil

100 ml (3 oz) canned coconut milk

1 tsp vanilla bean paste

40 g (⅜ cup) high-quality cocoa powder

200 g (1⅝ cups) self-rising flour

5 g (2 tsp) baking powder

⅓ tsp baking soda

1 tsp ground cinnamon

½ tsp mixed spice

Pinch of salt

40 g (2 oz) crushed vegan biscuits (I use Lotus Biscoff®)

S'mores Layer Cake (Continued)

While the cakes cool, prepare the frosting and meringue. For the frosting, beat the butter until pale and fluffy using an electric hand whisk or stand mixer at low to medium speed. Gradually add the powdered sugar and vanilla and continue to mix until fully incorporated.

For the vegan meringue topping, use an electric hand whisk at medium speed to beat the aquafaba until foamy and doubled in size. Add the cream of tartar and continue to whisk until stiff peaks are formed. This will take about 5 minutes.

Begin adding the powdered sugar 13 grams (1 tablespoon) at a time as you whisk the mixture. Repeat this until everything is fully incorporated and your meringue appears beautifully glossy.

To assemble the cake, begin by spreading a generous layer of frosting over one of the sponges, then carefully place the second on top and frost the second layer as well.

Melt the dark chocolate in a heatproof bowl over a saucepan of gently boiling water. Once melted, add the coconut oil for a runnier consistency.

Drizzle the melted chocolate around the edges of your cake, allowing it to fall over the sides to create that drip effect.

Take your meringue and pipe swirls or a pattern of your choice all over the top layer of the cake. You could also spread this for a more rustic effect if you'd prefer. Use a kitchen torch to toast the meringue until golden. Alternatively, you could place the cake under the broiler for a couple minutes, making sure to watch this closely to prevent from burning. Garnish with some additional shards of dark chocolate and crushed vegan cookies and serve!

FROSTING

180 g (¾ cup) vegan stick butter, room temperature

230 g (1⅛ cup) powdered sugar

½ tsp vanilla paste

MERINGUE

120 ml (4 oz) aquafaba

½ tsp cream of tartar

180 g (⅞ cup) powdered sugar

DRIZZLE

80 g (3 oz) vegan dark chocolate (extra to garnish)

1 tsp coconut oil

Crushed vegan cookies of choice

Gingerbread Latte Layer Cake

This Gingerbread Latte Layer Cake is everyone's favorite festive hot drink in cake form! It's sweet, spiced, creamy and has a healthy dose of rich coffee flavor! Despite looking incredibly impressive, this cake is simple to make and a perfect way to add a touch of festive indulgence to your coffee mornings. This is also one of my favorite recipes to take to work events or gift to friends during the festive season, so I can personally vouch that it always goes down as an absolute treat!

Preheat the oven to 355°F (180°C) and line three 6-inch (15-cm) loose-bottom cake pans with parchment paper.

In a mixing bowl, add the olive oil, superfine sugar and coconut palm sugar, and using a wooden spoon, beat until pale and fluffy. Pour in the oat milk, coconut milk, vanilla and coffee (fresh and instant, if using). Whisk these together to combine.

Sift the flour, baking powder and baking soda and fold these into your wet ingredients along with the mixed spice, ground ginger, cinnamon and pinch of salt.

Divide your mixture evenly among the three cake pans and bake for 30 minutes. Remove them from the oven and let them cool in the pans for 10 minutes before transferring to a wire rack.

(continued)

Yield: 10 Servings

CAKE
100 ml (4 oz) olive oil

150 g (¾ cup) superfine or granulated sugar

50 g (¼ cup) coconut palm sugar

100 ml (3 oz) oat milk

100 ml (3 oz) canned coconut milk

1 tsp vanilla bean paste

40 ml (1 oz) fresh-brewed coffee

2–4 g (1–2 tsp) instant coffee mixed with 1 tsp water (optional)

310 g (2½ cups) self-rising flour

5 g (2 tsp) baking powder

⅓ tsp baking soda

½ tsp mixed spice

½ tsp ground ginger

1 tsp ground cinnamon

Pinch of salt

Gingerbread Latte Layer Cake (Continued)

Meanwhile, for the frosting, beat the butter for 3 to 5 minutes, until pale and fluffy. You can do this using an electric hand whisk or stand mixer at medium speed.

Gradually add the powdered sugar while continuing to whisk to fully combine. Once the buttercream is perfectly smooth and creamy, fold in the vanilla and cinnamon.

To assemble your cake, spread or pipe a layer of frosting onto one of your cake layers, then carefully place the second on top. Repeat this step with the third layer, then top your cake with the remaining frosting, reserving some for decorating.

I love to garnish this with buttercream swirls, a simple sprinkling of cinnamon sugar and some mini gingerbread men.

FROSTING

250 g (1¹⁄₁₀ cups) vegan stick butter

300 g (1½ cups) powdered sugar

1 tsp vanilla bean paste

½ tsp ground cinnamon

TOPPINGS

Cinnamon sugar

Vegan gingerbread men

Coffee Lovers Caramel Drip Cake

As you can guess from the title, this cake is dedicated to all the coffee lovers out there, including me! This cake has two layers of moist coffee-infused sponge cake that are gloriously sandwiched together and coated with a vanilla coffee buttercream frosting and a generous drizzle of homemade coffee caramel sauce.

Preheat your oven to 355°F (180°C) and line two 6½-inch (17-cm) loose-bottom cake pans with parchment paper.

To make the vegan buttermilk alternative, add the apple cider vinegar to the soy milk, stir and let thicken for 5 minutes.

Mix the light brown sugar, butter, olive oil and sugar until pale and fluffy. Pour in the buttermilk, vanilla and coffee and mix well.

Sift the self-rising flour, baking powder and baking soda into the mixing bowl and fold the wet and dry ingredients together.

Once the batter is nice and smooth, divide it evenly between your two cake pans and bake for 30 to 35 minutes, until golden and well risen.

While the cakes are cooling, you can make your frosting. Beat the butter using an electric hand whisk or stand mixer on low to medium speed until pale and fluffy. Add the coffee. Continue beating while gradually adding the powdered sugar until fully combined and you're left with a super thick, creamy frosting.

To assemble your cake, start by spreading an even buttercream layer over one of the sponge cakes. Make a small dip in the center to help prevent the filling from spilling over the sides and fill with 45 to 60 milliliters (3 to 4 tablespoons) of homemade vegan caramel. Carefully place your second cake layer on top.

Take two-thirds of your remaining frosting and smooth this over the entire cake to cover. Use a cake scraper and palette knife to create an even finish. Refrigerate for 5 to 10 minutes.

Pour the leftover vegan caramel over the top of your cake. Smooth over the edges using an offset spatula to create a drip effect. Fill a piping bag with the remaining frosting and pipe decorative swirls around the edge to finish and top with coffee beans.

Yield: 8–10 Servings

CAKE
15 ml (1 tbsp) apple cider vinegar

150 ml (5 oz) soy milk

60 g (⅓ cup) light brown sugar

30 g (2 tbsp) vegan butter

60 ml (2 oz) olive oil

140 g (⅔ cup) superfine or granulated sugar

Dash of vanilla extract

100 ml (3 oz) freshly brewed coffee

310 g (2½ cups) self-rising flour

5 g (2 tsp) baking powder

⅓ tsp baking soda

1 batch homemade vegan caramel (see page 43)

FROSTING
250 g (1¹⁄₁₀ cups) vegan stick butter, at room temperature

1 tsp instant coffee mixed with 1 tsp hot water

300 g (1½ cups) powdered sugar

Coffee beans, for garnish

Single-Tier & Sheet Cakes

This collection of my most loved single-tier and sheet cakes is perfect if you're looking for something easy to make without compromising on delicious indulgence! All these recipes can be made in less than an hour and are easy to assemble and decorate.

Sheet cakes are a fantastic way to indulge in some of your favorite cake classics without having the fuss of baking an entire layer cake. Most of my sheet cake recipes can be made using one bowl and are ideal for sharing. They're distinguished enough to serve for a special occasion, yet simple enough to bake for your everyday dessert!

There's such a variety of flavor combinations in this chapter, so whether you fancy something fresh and fruity or layers of triple chocolate decadence, there's a recipe here for you! A recipe you simply can't miss is the Vegan Sticky Toffee Pudding (page 77)! This is simply an all-around winner for any occasion with a soft, fluffy sponge cake and luxurious spiced caramel sauce. It's incredible paired with a scoop of coconut ice cream!

PB & J Sheet Cake

I don't know if there's a more iconic flavor combination than peanut butter and jelly! I just love the contrast of the salty, nutty flavor and sweet vibrant berries. If you're an avid peanut butter lover, you're going to want to give this cake a try! This is a light and fluffy peanut butter sponge cake, topped with a slightly tangy berry jelly layer and the dreamiest topping of peanut butter buttercream frosting. This is such a decadent treat and will be a guaranteed crowd-pleaser among your friends and family!

Preheat your oven to 355°F (180°C) and line a 9-inch (23-cm) baking pan with parchment paper.

To make the vegan buttermilk alternative, add the apple cider vinegar to the soy milk, stir and let thicken for 5 minutes.

In a large mixing bowl, cream together the olive oil, peanut butter and sugar until pale and fluffy. Pour in the buttermilk and vanilla and whisk to fully combine.

Sift the flour, baking powder, baking soda and salt and carefully fold these into the wet mixture to form a smooth cake batter.

Pour the batter into your baking pan and bake for 35 minutes, until the cake is cooked through and beautifully risen.

Meanwhile, prepare your jelly layer. In a saucepan over low to medium heat, gently simmer the berries with a splash of water. Once the berries have started to break down and release some of the wonderful juices, remove them from the burner.

Add the jelly into a mixing jug with the boiling water and cold water and stir to dissolve. Add the stewed berries, then let the mixture cool.

Pour the jelly mixture over the sponge cake layer and refrigerate for 3 hours to allow it to set.

(continued)

Yield: 8-10 Servings

CAKE

15 ml (1 tbsp) apple cider vinegar

170 ml (6 oz) soy milk

60 ml (2 oz) olive oil

60 g (¼ cup) smooth peanut butter

200 g (1 cup) golden superfine or granulated sugar

Dash of vanilla extract

240 g (1⅞ cups) self-rising flour

2 tsp baking powder

⅓ tsp baking soda

Pinch of salt

JELLY LAYER

300 g (2¼ cups) fresh or frozen mixed berries

12 g (0.5 oz) sugar-free berry-flavored jelly sachet

150 ml (5 oz) boiling water

200 ml (8 oz) cold water

To make the frosting, using either a stand mixer or electric hand whisk on low to medium speed, beat the butter until pale and fluffy.

Gradually add the powdered sugar while continuing to whisk and then add the peanut butter. Once you're left with a deliciously smooth and creamy frosting, add this to a piping bag fitted with a star-tip nozzle. Pipe the frosting onto the cake and top with a sprinkling of chopped peanuts, fresh raspberries and fresh pomegranate seeds.

FROSTING

200 g (⅞ cup) vegan stick butter, room temperature

250 g (1¼ cups) powdered sugar

2 tbsp smooth peanut butter

TOPPING

50 g (¼ cup) chopped peanuts

150 g (1 cup) fresh raspberries

100 g (4 oz) fresh pomegranate seeds

Torched Lemon Meringue Sheet Cake

This is perhaps one of the more decadent of the sheet cakes, but it is completely worth the extra time and effort! A layer of sweet lemon sponge cake is topped with a tart homemade lemon curd and soft, marshmallowy freshly torched meringue. It's sweet, vibrant and delicate all in one mouthful and is honestly so delicious! I also can't deny that torching your meringue is rather a lot of fun! This is a great dessert for any citrus fan or if you're looking to impress guests with something a little fancier.

Preheat your oven to 355°F (180°C) and line a 9-inch (23-cm) baking dish with parchment paper.

To make the vegan buttermilk alternative, add the lemon juice to the soy milk, stir and let thicken for 5 minutes.

In a mixing bowl, combine the sugar and lemon zest and rub these together using your fingers to infuse the sugar with the citrus flavor. Pour in the olive oil and mix it into the sugar.

Stir in the buttermilk, yogurt and lemon juice, then sift in the self-rising flour, baking powder, baking soda and a pinch of salt. Fold the wet and dry ingredients together, then pour into your lined tray.

Bake in the oven for 30 minutes, then allow to cool completely.

While the cake is baking, make the lemon curd. Add the lemon juice, zest, almond milk and sugar to a saucepan. Heat over medium heat to allow the sugar to dissolve. Whisk in your corn starch and bring to a boil; reduce to a simmer for 5 minutes as the mixture thickens. Remove from the heat and allow it to cool.

Spread the lemon curd over your sponge cake and refrigerate for 1 hour to set.

(continued)

Yield: 8-10 Servings

CAKE
15 ml (1 tbsp) lemon juice

150 ml (5 oz) soy milk

150 g (¾ cup) superfine or granulated sugar

Zest from 2 lemons

60 ml (2 oz) olive oil

45 g (¼ cup) plant-based yogurt (soy works best)

Juice from 1 lemon

200 g (1⅝ cups) self-rising flour

5 g (2 tsp) baking power

⅓ tsp baking soda

Pinch of salt

LEMON CURD
Juice from 2 lemons

Zest from 2 lemons

110 ml (3 oz) almond milk

100 g (½ cup) superfine or granulated sugar

9 g (3 tsp) corn starch

Torched Lemon Meringue Sheet Cake (Continued)

To make the meringue topping, add the aquafaba to a clean, dry mixing bowl and whisk using an electric hand mixer on medium speed until the aquafaba has doubled in size. Add the cream of tartar and continue whisking to form stiff peaks.

Gradually add the powdered sugar as you mix, so that you're left with a luxuriously glossy meringue. Spread this over the lemon curd layer using a palette knife to create a swirled pattern. Use a kitchen torch to toast the meringue until golden. Alternatively, you could place this under a broiler for a couple of minutes to toast, but keep a close eye on it.

To garnish, I love to finish these off with a swirl of vegan whipped cream and a slice of fresh lemon.

MERINGUE LAYER

120 ml (4 oz) aquafaba

½ tsp cream of tartar

180 g (⅞ cup) powdered sugar

TOPPING

Vegan whipped cream

Fresh lemon slices

Vegan Sticky Toffee Pudding

No baker's recipe collection is complete without an ultimate sticky toffee pudding recipe! My Vegan Sticky Toffee Pudding is sweet, moist and the perfect ending to any dinner party! This recipe is wonderfully simple to make and something I find myself craving at least once a week!

Preheat the oven to 355°F (180°C) and line an 8-inch (20-cm) baking pan with parchment paper.

To make the vegan buttermilk alternative, add the apple cider vinegar to the soy milk, stir and let thicken for 5 minutes.

Place the chopped dates into a bowl of boiling water to soak.

In a large mixing bowl, pour in the sugar and olive oil and mix with a wooden spoon. Pour in the buttermilk and roughly whisk it in.

Add the self-rising flour, baking powder, salt, cinnamon, ginger and mixed spice and fold them into your wet mixture to fully combine. Drain the dates and stir these through the cake batter.

Pour the batter into the lined pan and bake for 30 minutes.

Meanwhile, to prepare the toffee sauce, gently heat your milk in a saucepan and whisk in your almond butter, maple syrup, brown sugar, cinnamon and salt. Remove from the heat once fully combined. You can add a little extra milk if your sauce is too thick. You're aiming for a runny, pourable consistency.

Once your cake is ready, remove it from the oven and use a fork to pierce the cake throughout. Drizzle over half of your toffee sauce and allow this to soak through.

Allow it to cool slightly for 10 minutes before slicing into portions. To serve, you can gently reheat the toffee sauce and drizzle a little extra over the top! I also love adding a scoop of nondairy ice cream!

Yield: 6–8 Servings

CAKE

15 ml (1 tbsp) apple cider vinegar

200 ml (7 oz) soy milk

80 g (½ cup) pitted dates, chopped

180 g (⅞ cup) superfine or granulated sugar

60 ml (2 oz) olive oil

210 g (1⅔ cups) self-rising flour

5 g (2 tsp) baking powder

Pinch of salt

1 tsp ground cinnamon

¼ tsp ground ginger

½ tsp mixed spice

CARAMEL TOFFEE SAUCE

180 ml (6 oz) plant-based milk

32 g (2 tbsp) smooth almond butter

30 ml (2 tbsp) maple syrup

23 g (2 tbsp) brown sugar

½ tsp ground cinnamon

Pinch of salt

Nondairy ice cream (optional)

Triple Chocolate Sheet Cake

I firmly believe that this cake is the key to any chocolate lover's heart. This is such a quick and simple recipe that's perfect for birthdays, bake sales, dinners with friends or simply to satisfy some late-evening chocolate cravings!

Preheat your oven to 375°F (190°C) and line a 9-inch (23-cm) brownie tray with parchment paper.

To make the vegan buttermilk alternative, add the apple cider vinegar to the soy milk, stir and let thicken for 5 minutes.

In a large mixing bowl, add the olive oil, brown sugar and superfine sugar and mix well until pale and fluffy. Stir in the soy yogurt and buttermilk, then sift the flour, cocoa powder, salt, baking powder and baking soda and fold these into the wet mixture.

Once you're left with a smooth, chocolaty batter, mix in your chopped chocolates and transfer this to your cake pan.

Bake for 25 to 30 minutes, then remove from the oven and allow to cool.

While the cake is cooling, you can prepare the frosting. Start by using an electric hand whisk or stand mixer on low to medium speed to beat the butter and cream cheese together for a few minutes, until pale and fluffy.

Gradually add the powdered sugar and cocoa powder while mixing until fully combined and you're left with an ultra-creamy frosting.

When your cake has completely cooled, spread or pipe the frosting over it and slice into portions. You can serve these as they are or top with some berries, pomegranate seeds and mint.

Yield: 8-10 Servings

CAKE
15 ml (1 tbsp) apple cider vinegar

185 ml (6 oz) soy milk

60 ml (2 oz) olive oil

80 g (½ cup) brown sugar

50 g (¼ cup) sugar

50 g (¼ cup) soy yogurt

150 g (1¼ cup) self-rising flour

35 g (⅓ cup) cocoa powder

Pinch of salt

1 tsp baking powder

⅓ tsp baking soda

45 g (¼ cup) vegan dark chocolate, chopped

45 g (¼ cup) vegan milk chocolate, chopped

FROSTING
100 g (¼ cup) vegan butter

100 g (½ cup) vegan cream cheese

250 g (1¼ cups) powdered sugar

30 g (¼ cup) cocoa powder

TOPPING
Fresh berries and pomegranate seeds

Fresh mint leaves

Crinkle-Top Brownies

People are either cakey or fudgy brownie lovers . . . I am firmly in favor of the latter! For me, the ultimate brownie has a crinkled top, rich chocolate flavor, ultra-gooey texture and an extremely generous helping of chocolate chunks! As well as, of course, being completely plant based, these brownies tick each of those boxes and are one to bake for any friends who are still skeptical of vegan baking! Although I should probably warn you, once you've made these, I doubt you'll be wanting to share!

Preheat the oven to 355°F (180°C) and line a 9-inch (23-cm) brownie pan with parchment paper.

Begin by melting your dark chocolate, milk chocolate, sugars and butter together in a heatproof bowl placed over a pan of gently boiling water.

Once the chocolate has melted and the sugars have dissolved, whisk in the milk.

In a separate bowl, sift the self-rising flour and cocoa powder. Pour in the wet ingredients and add a pinch of salt, then fold until you're left with a silky-smooth batter. I then like to whisk the mixture well for about 30 seconds, as this is what will help to achieve that crackly top!

Stir in the chopped chocolate and pour the batter into your brownie pan. Bake for 20 to 25 minutes, then remove from the oven and allow to cool. The brownies should still be quite soft and appear slightly undercooked, but they will firm up as they cool!

For an extra special finishing touch, I love adding a drizzle of melted chocolate and some fresh blueberries and garnishing with fresh mint and star anise.

Yield: 8-10 Servings

100 g (4 oz) vegan dark chocolate

75 g (3 oz) vegan milk chocolate

60 g (⅓ cup) soft brown sugar

56 g (⅓ cup) golden superfine sugar

65 g (¼ cup) vegan stick butter

75 ml (⅓ cup) nondairy milk

100 g (⁸∕₁₀ cup) self-rising flour

30 g (¼ cup) high-quality cocoa powder

Pinch of salt

50 g (2 oz) vegan milk or dark chocolate, chopped

TOPPING

Melted chocolate

Fresh blueberries or other berries of choice

Fresh mint

Star anise

Carrot Sheet Cake with Cream Cheese Frosting

This is an incredibly easy and delicious carrot cake recipe with what I believe is simply the best cream cheese frosting! People seriously won't believe that this recipe is completely plant based! The sponge cake is lightly spiced, incredibly moist and has a little added crunch from the pecans and coconut. If you don't have the time or energy to prepare a layer cake, this sheet cake is the perfect solution to your dessert needs!

Preheat your oven to 355°F (180°C) and line a 9-inch (23-cm) brownie tray with parchment paper.

To make the vegan buttermilk alternative, add the apple cider vinegar to the soy milk, stir and let thicken for 5 minutes.

Cream the sugar and olive oil together until slightly pale, then whisk in the buttermilk mixture.

Sift the self-rising flour, baking powder and baking soda. Fold these into the wet mixture, along with the cinnamon, salt, coconut and pecans. Add the orange zest and grated carrot and mix well.

Transfer this into your baking pan and bake for 30 minutes, then remove from the oven and allow to cool.

For the cream cheese frosting, use an electric hand whisk or stand mixer on low to medium speed to beat the cream cheese and butter together until smooth and creamy. Continue mixing while gradually adding in the powdered sugar until fully combined.

Spread this over your sheet cake and slice into portions. Garnish with some fresh orange slices and serve.

Yield: 8-10 Servings

CAKE

15 ml (1 tbsp) apple cider vinegar

200 ml (7 oz) soy milk

150 g (¾ cup) superfine or granulated sugar

75 ml (3 oz) olive oil

250 g (2 cups) self-rising flour

5 g (2 tsp) baking powder

⅓ tsp baking soda

1 tsp ground cinnamon

Pinch of salt

40 g (½ cup) desiccated coconut

30 g (¼ cup) chopped pecans

Zest from 1 orange

100 g (1 cup) grated carrot

CREAM CHEESE FROSTING

100 g (½ cup) vegan cream cheese

100 g (½ cup) vegan stick butter, room temperature

250 g (1¼ cup) powdered sugar

Fresh orange slices, for topping

Strawberry Swirl Cake

My favorite thing about this Strawberry Swirl Cake is that it's made with 200 grams (1 cup) of fresh strawberries! They add moisture and a beautiful pink color to the cake, as well as an incredible fresh strawberry flavor. I love to add freeze-dried strawberries to the mixture for a more intense berry flavor! This light and fruity sponge is so simple to make and is perfect if you're after something with a more delicate, fresh flavor. This recipe can be made in one bowl, requiring only a few simple steps and is something that everybody is going to enjoy!

Preheat the oven to 355°F (180°C) and line a 9-inch (23-cm) baking dish with parchment paper.

To make the vegan buttermilk alternative, add the apple cider vinegar to the almond milk, stir and let thicken for 5 minutes.

Add the sugar and olive oil to a mixing bowl, then cream these together using a wooden spoon or electric hand mixer.

Remove the strawberry tops and pop the rinsed berries into the blender and blitz to a puree. Pour the buttermilk, blended strawberries and vanilla into your bowl and mix well.

Sift the self-rising flour, baking powder and baking soda, then fold the wet and dry ingredients together until fully combined. Divide your batter into two portions and add a few drops of pink food coloring into one of the portions.

Spread one of the cake mixtures into your lined dish, then add dollops of the second color throughout. Use a knife to swirl these together, then place into the oven to bake for 30 minutes.

Once cooked, remove from the oven and allow to cool completely. Meanwhile, for the frosting, whisk your cream to soft peaks, then gradually add the powdered sugar, while continuing to whisk. You can add a few drops of pink food coloring for a colored frosting if you would like.

Lather the frosting over the cooled cake and top with the fresh strawberries and pomegranate seeds.

Yield: 8-10 Servings

CAKE
15 ml (1 tbsp) apple cider vinegar

80 ml (3 oz) almond milk

125 g (5/8 cup) superfine or granulated sugar

60 ml (2 oz) light, mild olive oil

200 g (1 cup) strawberries

Dash of vanilla extract

210 g (1⅔ cups) self-rising flour

2 tsp baking powder

⅓ tsp baking soda

A few drops of vegan-friendly pink food coloring

FROSTING
250 ml (1 cup) vegan whipping cream

38 g (3 tbsp) powdered sugar

A few drops of vegan-friendly pink food coloring (optional)

TOPPING
250 g (1¼ cup) fresh strawberries

100 g (4 oz) fresh pomegranate seeds

Orange Upside-Down Cake

This Orange Upside-Down Cake is one of my favorite simple recipes for any occasion and I'm so excited to share it with you! A light and delicate sponge cake, infused with the vibrant tangy notes of orange, is perfect if you're after something sweet but slightly lighter. By layering the oranges at the base of your cake pan, it creates this glorious, caramelized topping and allows all the divine syrupy juices to soak into the sponge.

Preheat your oven to 355°F (180°C) and line an 7-inch (18-cm) springform cake pan with parchment paper.

In a saucepan, combine the water and sugar and simmer over medium heat for 5 minutes to create a syrup. Slice both oranges into thin pieces (there's no need to remove the skin, but you can if you would prefer) and leave these to soak in the sugar syrup.

To make the vegan buttermilk alternative, add the apple cider vinegar to the soy milk, stir and let thicken for 5 minutes.

For the cake, start by rubbing the sugar and orange zest together with your fingers. Add the olive oil and beat these together using a wooden spoon. Stir in the buttermilk and yogurt, then add the self-rising flour, oat flour, baking powder and baking soda and carefully fold the wet and dry ingredients together.

Take the orange slices out of the syrup mixture and arrange them in the base of your cake pan. Pour the batter over the top and bake this for 45 to 50 minutes, until your cake is cooked through.

Allow the cake to cool before flipping the cake, slicing and serving. You can serve the cake as it is—the orange topping looks beautiful on it's own. Alternatively, you can also garnish with some fresh seasonal berries!

Yield: 8-10 Servings

SYRUP-SOAKED ORANGES

45 ml (3 tbsp) water

38 g (3 tbsp) superfine or granulated sugar

2 oranges

CAKE

15 ml (1 tbsp) apple cider vinegar

130 ml (4 oz) soy milk

180 g (⅞ cups) superfine or granulated sugar

Zest from 3 oranges

85 ml (3 oz) olive oil

50 g (¼ cup) soy yogurt

180 g (1½ cups) self-rising flour

45 g (½ cup) oat flour

5 g (2 tsp) baking powder

⅓ tsp baking soda

OPTIONAL TOPPING

Fresh seasonal berries

Caramelized Banana Sheet Cake

While appearing rather impressive, this Caramelized Banana Sheet Cake is surprisingly simple to make! This is another one-bowl recipe that requires minimal prep and kitchen time! However, it's guaranteed to impress those eating it, and they'll never guess just how easy it was!

Preheat your oven to 355°F (180°C) and line a 9-inch (23-cm) baking dish with parchment paper.

To make the vegan buttermilk alternative, add the apple cider vinegar to the almond milk, stir and let thicken for 5 minutes.

To make the caramel, begin by heating the brown sugar and water in a saucepan and bring to a boil. Swirl the sugar and water together by moving the pan if needed and avoid stirring with a spoon to prevent burning.

Reduce the heat to medium-low and allow the mixture to bubble and the sugar to dissolve. Stir in the cashew butter to combine and form a smooth caramel mixture.

To form the amazing caramelized banana topping, slice your bananas in half lengthwise and arrange these cut side down onto the base of your baking dish. Pour the glorious, nutty caramel over the bananas and set aside.

For the cake, in a large mixing bowl, add the sugar and olive oil and beat these together using a wooden spoon. Stir in the plant-based yogurt and buttermilk.

Once combined, fold in the flour, ground almonds, cinnamon, vanilla, baking powder and baking soda until your cake batter is nice and smooth.

Pour this over the glorious caramel-coated banana layer and bake in the oven for 40 to 45 minutes.

Remove the cake from the oven and allow it to cool completely. Carefully flip your cake onto a serving board and peel away the paper to reveal the beautiful caramelized banana top! This is delicious served hot or cold and I love adding a scoop of vegan ice cream for a little extra indulgence!

Yield: 8–10 Servings

CAKE

15 ml (1 tbsp) apple cider vinegar

125 ml (½ cup) almond milk

190 g (⅞ cup) superfine or granulated sugar

100 ml (4 oz) olive oil

100 g (½ cup) plant-based yogurt (soy, coconut or almond would work)

200 g (1⅝ cups) self-rising flour

30 g (¼ cup) ground almonds

¾ tsp ground cinnamon

Dash of vanilla extract

5 g (2 tsp) baking powder

⅓ tsp baking soda

CARAMEL

40 g (4 tbsp) brown sugar

60 ml (4 tbsp) water

16 g (1 tbsp) cashew or almond butter

3 bananas

Vegan ice cream, optional

Pistachio & Vanilla Bean Sheet Cake

This is my go-to one-pan bake for when I'm in the mood for something light and delicate to satisfy those sweet cravings! It's the perfect pairing for an afternoon tea or lunchtime dessert and a firm favorite during the spring and summer months! Vanilla bean and pistachio are the perfect, subtle flavor pairings, especially when accompanied by a glorious whipped cream topping!

Preheat your oven to 355°F (180°C) and line a 9-inch (20-cm) baking dish with parchment paper.

To make the vegan buttermilk alternative, add the apple cider vinegar to the soy milk, stir and let thicken for 5 minutes.

In a mixing bowl, cream together the butter, olive oil and sugar using a wooden spoon or electric hand whisk on low to medium speed.

Whisk in the plant-based yogurt and buttermilk to fully combine. Slice open and scrape the inside of the vanilla pod and add the beans along with the self-rising flour, baking powder, salt and baking soda to the bowl.

Gently fold everything together and, lastly, add the finely ground pistachios.

Transfer the batter into the pan and bake for 30 minutes. You'll know your cake is cooked through when you can pierce it with a toothpick and this comes out clean. Once your cake is ready, allow it to cool completely while you prepare the topping.

Beat the whipping cream to soft peaks and add the powdered sugar while continuing to whisk.

Spread this over the cooled cake and garnish with an extra sprinkling of chopped pistachios.

Yield: 8–10 Servings

CAKE

15 ml (1 tbsp) apple cider vinegar

150 ml (5 oz) soy milk

40 g (⅛ cup) vegan butter

20 ml (0.5 oz) olive oil

150 g (¾ cup) superfine or granulated sugar

60 g (¼ cup) plant-based yogurt

1 vanilla pod

230 g (1⅞ cup) self-rising flour

5 g (2 tsp) baking powder

Pinch of salt

⅓ tsp baking soda

75 g (½ cup) pistachio nuts, finely ground

WHIPPED CREAM TOPPING

250 ml (1 cup) vegan whipping cream

25–38 g (2–3 tbsp) powdered sugar

GARNISH

50 g (⅓ cup) chopped pistachios

Cupcakes & Minis

This chapter is very special to me. It reminds me of how I began this journey. I always loved helping in the kitchen, looking through recipe magazines and cooking dishes to serve to friends and family.

My passion for baking developed at an early age, when I fell in love with baking and decorating cupcakes. I remember this not being for any specific event or purpose. I would simply make and decorate endless cupcakes and fairy cakes to de-stress and let my creativity flow. I apparently told my dad that I would love to be able to decorate cupcakes for a job when I grew up—at the time of course having no idea of the career I was yet to pursue!

I think the reason that I love cupcakes is because of how easy and versatile they are. Most of these recipes can be baked in 25 minutes or less with minimal preparation time. They're ideally suited for all occasions, from birthday celebrations to times when you simply fancy prepping a supply of single-serve sweet treats for the week!

I've tried to include the best array of cupcake flavors and frostings in this chapter that I possibly could. There's everything from decadent Double Chocolate Cupcakes (page 96) to the most incredible Browned-Butter Chai Cupcakes (page 95)! I can't wait for you to try these recipes and hope you love them just as much as I do!

Browned-Butter Chai Cupcakes

The only thing I could think of to top my classic chai cupcakes would be these Browned-Butter Chai Cupcakes. I don't know why, but everything just seems to be better with browned butter! The cupcakes themselves are perfectly fluffy and flavored with the glorious notes of warming chai spices and rich, nutty browned butter. You're going to love them!

Preheat your oven to 355°F (180°C) and prepare a muffin tray with cupcake liners.

To make the vegan buttermilk alternative, add the apple cider vinegar to the soy milk, stir and let thicken for 5 minutes.

Begin by browning the butter. Heat the butter in a saucepan over medium heat and continue to stir as the butter melts to ensure it keeps moving. Once the butter has started to foam at the edges, continue to heat for about 5 minutes, until golden brown.

In a large mixing bowl, add the sugar and beat together with the browed butter. Whisk in the buttermilk, then pour in the self-rising flour, oat flour, baking powder, cinnamon, mixed spice, ginger, cardamom and salt. Fold the wet and dry ingredients together until fully combined.

Use an ice-cream scoop to evenly divide the mixture among the cupcake liners and fill each of them three-fourths of the way up. Bake for 24 minutes, then remove and allow to cool.

Meanwhile, for the frosting, begin by beating the butter using an electric hand whisk or stand mixer on low to medium speed until pale and fluffy. Continue to whisk while gradually adding in the powdered sugar, cinnamon and ginger.

Add the frosting to a piping bag with a star-tip nozzle and pipe the frosting onto your cooled cupcakes. I love to finish these with a dusting of cinnamon sugar, a cinnamon stick and star anise in the center.

Yield: 7 Cupcakes

CUPCAKES

15 ml (1 tbsp) apple cider vinegar

125 ml (½ cup) soy milk

65 g (¼ cup) vegan stick butter

140 g (⅔ cup) golden superfine or granulated sugar

110 g (⅞ cup) self-rising flour

40 g (⅓ cup) oat flour

4 g (1 ½ tsp) baking powder

1 tsp ground cinnamon

½ tsp mixed spice

¼ tsp ground ginger

Pinch of ground cardamom

Pinch of salt

FROSTING

250 g (1¹⁄₁₀ cups) vegan stick butter, room temperature

300 g (1½ cups) powdered sugar

½ tsp ground cinnamon

Pinch of ground ginger

TOPPING

Cinnamon sticks

Cinnamon sugar

Star anise

Double Chocolate Cupcakes with Whipped Frosting

These are the perfect chocolate cupcakes; they're super moist, rich and have a lovely bouncy texture. They're also studded with chocolate chips and topped with an extremely generous helping of this whipped chocolate frosting. This frosting uses a combination of melted chocolate and vegan whipped cream to achieve that ultra-smooth, silky consistency. This recipe takes under an hour to make, for a delicious chocolate fix without the hard work!

Preheat your oven to 355°F (180°C) and prepare a muffin tray with cupcakes liners.

To make the vegan buttermilk alternative, add the apple cider vinegar to the soy milk, stir and let thicken for 5 minutes.

Meanwhile, in a large mixing bowl, beat the butter and sugar together using a wooden spoon or electric hand whisk on medium speed until pale and fluffy. Pour in the buttermilk and yogurt and mix until well combined.

Sift the flour, cocoa powder, baking powder and baking soda and add them to the wet ingredients along with a good pinch of salt.

Gently fold the ingredients together and then transfer the cupcake batter into the liners. I like to use an ice-cream scoop to help divide the batter evenly. You want to fill each liner approximately three-fourths.

Bake for 23 to 25 minutes, then remove from the oven and allow to cool on a wire rack.

In the meantime, prepare the frosting. Begin by melting the chocolate in a heatproof bowl over a pan of gently boiling water. Once melted, use a whisk to mix in the cream and powdered sugar to fully combine. You should be left with a smooth, glossy consistency.

To frost the cakes, you can either pipe swirls or spread the luxurious chocolate frosting over the cooled cupcakes using a palette knife. Decorate with the fresh berries, dark chocolate and fresh mint!

Yield: 6-7 Cupcakes

CUPCAKES
15 ml (1 tbsp) apple cider vinegar

110 ml (4 oz) soy milk

60 g (¼ cup) vegan butter

150 g (¾ cup) superfine or granulated sugar

60 g (¼ cup) soy yogurt

100 g (⅘ cup) self-rising flour

30 g (¼ cup) high-quality cocoa powder

1 tsp baking powder

⅓ tsp baking soda

Generous pinch of salt

FROSTING
150 g (1 cup) vegan chocolate (dark or milk)

270 ml (1 cup) vegan whipping cream

60 g (½ cup) powdered sugar

TOPPING
250 g (1 cup) fresh berries

50 g (2 oz) vegan dark chocolate

Fresh mint

Fresh Strawberry Cupcakes

This was one of the first recipes written for this book and is still one of my firm favorites! After testing some initial ideas for these cupcakes, they were something that I instantly knew I wanted to include and share with you! The sponge mixture is made with real, fresh strawberries, creating the most delicious, moist texture and adding an unbeatable authentic strawberry flavor. Bursting with sweet notes of the strawberries, these cupcakes are the epitome of summertime desserts and are super light and fluffy! This recipe is also incredibly easy to make and is always considered a real treat!

Preheat your oven to 355°F (180°C). This recipe makes 16 cupcakes, so you will need 1½-lined muffin trays. You can halve the quantities to make a smaller batch if you would like.

To make the vegan buttermilk alternative, add the apple cider vinegar to the soy milk, stir and let thicken for 5 minutes.

Pop the strawberries into a blender or food processor and blitz them to make a puree.

In a large mixing bowl or stand mixer, add the sugar and olive oil and beat these until slightly pale. Stir in the buttermilk, vanilla and strawberry puree.

Sift the flour, baking powder and baking soda into the mixing bowl and fold these into the wet ingredients along with a pinch of salt and the lime zest.

Once fully combined and the batter is nice and smooth, add a pinch of beetroot powder or a few drops of vegan-friendly food coloring, if desired, to enhance the pink color.

Using an ice-cream scoop, evenly divide the mixture among the cupcake liners and place them into the oven to bake for approximately 20 minutes. Check to see if your cakes are ready by inserting a toothpick. If it comes out clean, the cakes are cooked through.

Transfer to a wire rack to allow these to cool while you make the frosting.

Yield: 16 Cupcakes

CUPCAKES

15 ml (1 tbsp) apple cider vinegar

125 ml (½ cup) soy milk

400 g (3¼ cups) fresh sliced strawberries

300 g (1½ cups) superfine or granulated sugar

118 ml (4 oz) olive oil

Dash of vanilla extract

300 g (2⅖ cups) plain flour

5 g (2 tsp) baking powder

½ tsp baking soda

Pinch of salt

Zest from 2 limes

Pinch of beetroot powder or vegan-friendly pink food coloring (optional)

FROSTING

310 g (1⅜ cups) vegan stick butter, room temperature

600 g (3 cups) powdered sugar

Vegan pink food coloring or beetroot powder

For the frosting, using either a stand mixer or electric hand whisk, start by beating the butter until it is super pale and fluffy. Gradually add the powdered sugar while continuing to mix and repeat this until it's fully incorporated.

Add a few drops of the food coloring and beat again until you've achieved the desired shade of pink. Transfer the frosting into a piping bag. I like to use a star-tip nozzle for this but you can use any tip! Pipe the frosting onto each of the cupcakes and top with some freeze-dried strawberry pieces berries and pomegranate seeds.

TOPPING
10 g (0.75 oz) freeze-dried strawberry pieces

Fresh berries

Fresh pomegranate seeds

Lotus Biscoff® Cupcakes

These Lotus Biscoff® Cupcakes are the perfect cake for any time of day, any day of the week! If you're a fan of Biscoff, then these are going to be a dream come true! This is a moist and fluffy Biscoff-flavored cupcake, filled with a creamy center and then topped with the most incredible Biscoff frosting.

Preheat your oven to 355°F (180°C) and prepare a muffin tray with cupcake liners.

To make the vegan buttermilk alternative, add the apple cider vinegar to the almond milk, stir and let thicken for 5 minutes.

In a mixing bowl, use a wooden spoon or electric hand whisk, beat the butter and sugar together until pale and fluffy. Add the Biscoff spread and mix to combine.

Stir in the buttermilk and vanilla, then sift in the flour, baking powder, baking soda and a pinch of salt. Fold the wet and dry ingredients together until smooth, then divide the batter among the cupcake liners.

Bake for 25 minutes, then remove from the oven and allow to cool completely.

Once cooled, remove the center of each cupcake (I recommend using an apple corer) and fill each well with a teaspoon of the cookie spread.

For the delicious Biscoff frosting, beat the butter until pale and fluffy. You can use either an electric hand whisk or stand mixer. Add the powdered sugar while continuing to whisk and then add the Biscoff spread. When the buttercream is ultra-creamy and smooth, transfer it into a piping bag fitted with a star-tip nozzle.

Pipe the frosting onto each of the cupcakes and top with a biscuit and a drizzle of melted Biscoff spread to finish.

Yield: 6-7 Cupcakes

CUPCAKES
15 ml (1 tbsp) apple cider vinegar

125 ml (½ cup) almond milk

50 g (⅕ cup) vegan butter

120 g (⅝ cup) golden superfine or granulated sugar

60 g (2 oz) smooth Lotus Biscoff spread

Dash of vanilla extract

135 g (1⅛) self-rising flour

1 tsp baking powder

½ tsp baking soda

Pinch of salt

FILLING
64 g (4 tbsp) Lotus Biscoff spread

FROSTING
250 g (1¹⁄₁₀ cups) vegan stick butter

300 g (1½ cups) powdered sugar

32 g (2 heaping tbsp) smooth Lotus Biscoff spread

TOPPING
Lotus Biscoff biscuits

Melted Biscoff spread

Funfetti® Cupcakes

These Funfetti® Cupcakes are a soft and fluffy classic vanilla cupcake with an extra finishing touch of rainbow sprinkles! I know sprinkles don't technically have a flavor, but I feel like funfetti is definitely a flavor of its own! They're the perfect birthday treat, no matter the theme or style of the occasion. These will never not be in fashion! What makes these even more delicious is a generous helping of creamy vegan buttercream frosting, and in this case, I think the more frosting, the better!

Preheat your oven to 347°F (175°C) and prepare a muffin pan with cupcake liners.

To make the vegan buttermilk alternative, add the apple cider vinegar to the soy milk, stir and let thicken for 5 minutes.

In a large mixing bowl, cream together the sugar and olive oil until slightly pale in color. Pour in the buttermilk and yogurt and mix these thoroughly.

Sift the self-rising flour, baking powder and baking soda and fold these carefully into the wet ingredients.

Once the batter is nice and smooth, stir in the rainbow sprinkles and divide the batter among the cupcake liners. I like to use an ice-cream scoop for this to help distribute the batter more evenly.

Bake these for 23 minutes, until lightly golden, then remove from the oven and allow to cool completely.

Meanwhile, for the frosting, add the butter to a bowl or stand mixer and beat until pale and fluffy. Gradually incorporate the powdered sugar and continue until the mixture reaches a super creamy consistency.

Transfer the frosting into a piping bag fitted with a nozzle of your choice and pipe a generous swirl of frosting onto each of the cakes. Garnish with some extra sprinkles and serve.

Yield: 7 Cupcakes

CUPCAKES

15 ml (1 tbsp) apple cider vinegar

120 ml (½ cup) soy milk

130 g (⅔ cups) superfine or granulated sugar

65 ml (4 tbsp + 1 tsp) olive oil (or other neutral oil of choice)

65 g (¼ cup) plant-based yogurt

170 g (1⅜ cups) self-rising flour

1 tsp baking powder

⅓ tsp baking soda

50 g (2 oz) rainbow sprinkles

FROSTING

250 g (1¹⁄₁₀ cups) vegan stick butter, room temperature

300 g (1½ cups) powdered sugar

TOPPING

Rainbow sprinkles

Easy Vanilla Cupcakes with Roasted Strawberries

These really are some of the simplest vanilla cupcakes that you'll ever bake. However, it doesn't mean you'll be compromising on taste! This is an easy, one-bowl recipe for divinely light and fluffy cupcakes, topped with a simple vanilla buttercream frosting and a glorious crown of sweet roasted strawberries.

Preheat your oven to 355°F (180°C) and prepare a muffin tray with cupcake liners.

Wash and slice the strawberries and place them into an oven-safe dish with the sugar, if using. Set aside; you're going to pop these in to roast at the same time as the cupcakes.

To make the vegan buttermilk alternative, add the lemon juice to the soy milk, stir and let thicken for 5 minutes.

In a large mixing bowl, start by creaming together the butter and sugar. Once you're left with a light and fluffy consistency, pour in the buttermilk, vanilla and yogurt and stir until combined.

Sift the self-rising flour and baking powder to remove any lumps and fold them into the wet mixture to create a smooth and airy batter.

I then like to use an ice-cream scoop to divide the batter evenly among the cupcake liners. Fill them three-fourths full and then place the cakes into the oven along with the strawberries to bake for 23 to 25 minutes.

Once your cakes are beautifully risen and slightly golden on top, transfer them to a wire rack to cool.

Meanwhile, for the frosting, use an electric whisk or hand mixer and beat the butter until pale and fluffy. Continue mixing while adding the sugar and vanilla.

When the cupcakes have fully cooled, spread a generous portion of the frosting onto each and top with some of your beautiful roasted strawberries, fresh mint and chopped pistachios.

Yield: 7–8 Cupcakes

TOPPINGS
250 g (1¼ cups) fresh strawberries

12 g (1 tbsp) superfine or granulated sugar (optional)

Fresh mint

Chopped pistachios

CUPCAKES
15 ml (1 tbsp) lemon juice

125 ml (½ cup) soy milk

60 g (¼ cup) vegan stick butter, room temperature

120 g (⅝ cup) superfine or granulated sugar

Dash of vanilla extract or paste

40 g (¼ cup) plant-based yogurt

160 g (1¼ cup) self-rising flour

1 tsp baking powder

FROSTING
250 g (1¹⁄₁₀ cups) vegan stick butter, room temperature

300 g (1½ cups) powdered sugar

Dash of vanilla extract or paste

Coconut Frosted White Chocolate Cupcakes

Coconut and white chocolate are an utterly dreamy combination that works so well in these delicate, fluffy cupcakes! A soft, vanilla-infused sponge with little chunks of white chocolate throughout is then topped with a silky-smooth coconut and white chocolate buttercream.

Preheat your oven to 355°F (180°C) and prepare a muffin pan with cupcake liners.

To make the vegan buttermilk alternative, add the apple cider vinegar to the soy milk, stir and let thicken for 5 minutes.

In a mixing bowl, combine the butter and sugar, then beat well using a wooden spoon until pale and fluffy. Stir in the buttermilk and vanilla.

Sift the self-rising flour, baking powder and baking soda and carefully fold these into the wet mixture until smooth and fully combined. Mix in the white chocolate chips and divide the batter among the cupcake liners.

Bake for 25 minutes, then remove and allow to cool completely on a wire rack.

Meanwhile, for the filling, melt the white chocolate over low heat and stir in the cream until fully combined. Remove the center of each of the cakes (I like to use an apple corer). Add a spoonful of the creamy filling into each well.

For the coconut frosting, begin by beating the butter using a stand mixer or electric hand whisk until pale and fluffy. Gradually whisk in the powdered sugar until fully combined and you're left with a super smooth buttercream. Stir in the desiccated coconut and transfer to a piping bag with a large star nozzle.

Pipe a swirl onto each of the cupcakes and serve. Place a square of vegan white chocolate into the center of each of the buttercream swirls, sprinkle over your desiccated coconut and finish with a drizzle of melted white chocolate.

 *Yield:* 7 Cupcakes

CUPCAKES
15 ml (1 tbsp) apple cider vinegar

120 ml (½ cup) soy milk

60 g (¼ cup) vegan butter

120 g (⅝ cup) sugar

Dash of vanilla extract

125 g (1 cup) self-rising flour

1 tsp baking powder

⅓ tsp baking soda

60 g (2 oz) vegan white chocolate chips, more if desired

FILLING
70 g (⅓ cup) vegan white chocolate

125 ml (4 oz) vegan cream

FROSTING
250 g (1¹/₁₀ cups) vegan stick butter, room temperature

300 g (1½ cups) powdered sugar

7 g (2 tbsp) desiccated coconut

TOPPING
100 g (4 oz) vegan white chocolate, plus more for drizzling

30 g (⅓ cup) desiccated coconut

Pink Velvet Cupcakes

These adorable Pink Velvet Cupcakes are super easy to make, fluffy and perfect for a Valentine's Day treat . . . or any occasion, really! This recipe can be made in one bowl and takes less than 30 minutes to bake. The cupcakes are a slightly more subtle version of the classic red velvet cupcake, but with a very similar flavor.

Preheat your oven to 355°F (180°C) and prepare a muffin tray with cupcake liners.

To make the vegan buttermilk alternative, add the apple cider vinegar to the soy milk, stir and let thicken for 5 minutes.

In a large mixing bowl, use a wooden spoon to cream together the sugar and olive oil until they are pale and fluffy. Then stir in the buttermilk, yogurt and vanilla.

Sift in the self-rising flour, baking powder, cocoa powder and baking soda and add a pinch of salt. Fold both the wet and dry ingredients together until you're left with a smooth batter. Mix in a few drops of the vegan pink food coloring.

Divide the batter evenly among the cupcake liners. I use an ice-cream scoop. Bake for 25 minutes, then remove and allow to cool on a wire rack.

For the cream cheese frosting, beat the butter and cream cheese together until thick and creamy. You can do this using an electric hand whisk or stand mixer at low to medium speed. Gradually add the powdered sugar while mixing and continue to do so until all the sugar is fully incorporated.

Transfer the mixture to a piping bag fitted with a star-tip nozzle and pipe a generous amount of frosting onto each of the cupcakes.

To finish, top each of the frosted cupcakes with some of the fresh raspberries. You can also add some pomegranate seeds or strawberries here if you fancy!

Yield: 8 Cupcakes

CUPCAKES

15 ml (1 tbsp) apple cider vinegar

115 ml (½ cup) soy milk

120 g (⅝ cup) sugar

60 ml (2 oz) olive oil

50 g (¼ cup) coconut yogurt

Dash of vanilla extract

150 g (1¼ cup) self-rising flour

1½ tsp baking powder

10 g (⁷⁄₂₀ oz) high-quality cocoa powder

⅓ tsp baking soda

Pinch of salt

Vegan pink food coloring

FROSTING

150 g (¾ cup) vegan stick butter, room temperature

100 g (½ cup) vegan cream cheese

300 g (1½ cups) powdered sugar

TOPPING

100 g (¾ cup) fresh raspberries

Additional seasonal berries, optional

Cinnamon Roll Cupcakes

Cinnamon rolls are an all-time favorite dessert for me and always have been! I'm especially obsessed with them during the autumn months because as soon as September hits, nothing can separate me from those warming spices! These are an easy and convenient way to make and enjoy these incredible swirls of deliciousness!

Preheat your oven to 355°F (180°C). Prepare a muffin tray with 9 or 10 cupcake liners.

In a large mixing bowl, combine the flour, cinnamon, ginger, nutmeg, sugar, salt and yeast. Roughly mix everything together using a wooden spoon.

Gently heat the apple cider vinegar, milk and butter together in a saucepan over a low to medium heat. Once the milk is warm, make a well in the center of the flour and pour in the liquid.

Start mixing from the center outward to gradually combine the wet and dry ingredients. Once everything has begun to come together to form a shaggy mixture, you can use your hands to work the mixture together to form a dough.

Knead the dough on a lightly floured surface for 5 to 10 minutes, until it is elastic. Mold into a ball and let it rise in a lightly greased bowl covered with a clean tea towel.

Meanwhile, to prepare the cinnamon filling, mix the vegan butter, brown sugar, 24 grams (2 tbsp) of sugar and cinnamon.

Once the dough has doubled in size, knock this back and knead for another couple of minutes before rolling out onto a floured surface. Once the dough is ⅛ inch (3 mm) thick, spread the filling all over the surface of the dough . Mix the remaining 36 grams (3 tbsp) of sugar with a pinch of cinnamon and sprinkle it over the filling.

Start with one of the longest edges nearest to you and carefully roll the dough away from you. Once firmly rolled, slice into nine to ten pieces and place them into the cupcake liners. Cover this with plastic wrap and leave to prove for an additional 45 minutes.

Bake for 30 minutes, or until golden, then to cool.

For the glaze, mix the sugar, vanilla and milk together and lightly brush it over each cupcake before serving.

Yield: 9–10 Cupcakes

CINNAMON ROLLS
405 g (3¼ cups) bread flour

1 tsp ground cinnamon

½ tsp ground ginger

Pinch of nutmeg

50 g (¼ cup) sugar

Pinch of salt

7 g (2¼ tsp) fast-acting yeast

15 ml (1 tbsp) apple cider vinegar or lemon juice

210 ml (7 oz) nondairy milk

60 g (¼ cup) vegan butter

FILLING
70 g (⅓ cup) vegan butter

100 g (½ cup) brown sugar

60 g (5 tbsp) superfine or granulated sugar

6 g (2 tsp) ground cinnamon, plus a pinch

GLAZE
200 g (1½ cups) powdered sugar

1 tsp vanilla bean paste

30–45 ml (2–3 tbsp) nondairy milk

Black Forest Cupcakes

If you feel like you could dive headfirst into a huge slice of Black Forest cake, but don't quite fancy spending the time assembling a layer cake, then these cupcakes are the answer! They have all the components of a Black Forest cake, but in an individually sized portion.

Preheat your oven to 355°F (180°C) and prepare a muffin tray with 7 cupcake liners.

To make the vegan buttermilk alternative, add the apple cider vinegar to the soy milk, stir and let thicken for 5 minutes.

Cream the olive oil and sugar together using a wooden spoon. Then, pour in the buttermilk, vanilla and yogurt and mix thoroughly. Sift the self-rising flour, cocoa powder, baking powder and baking soda and add these into your mixing bowl along with a good pinch of salt.

Fold the wet and dry ingredients together to fully combine. Add the chocolate chips and transfer the batter to the cupcake liners. Bake for 20 to 25 minutes, until cooked through, then transfer to a wire rack to cool.

Meanwhile, for the frosting, begin by beating the butter until pale and fluffy. You can use an electric hand whisk or a stand mixer. Gradually add the sugar and vanilla and continue to mix so that the buttercream is ultra-smooth and creamy. Transfer the frosting to a piping bag fitted with a star-tip nozzle.

Once cooled, make a hole in the center of each cupcake (I use an apple corer) and fill with a teaspoon of the cherry jam. Top each of the cupcakes with a swirl of frosting, some of the grated dark chocolate and a cherry to finish.

Yield: 7 Cupcakes

CUPCAKES
15 ml (1 tbsp) apple cider vinegar

125 ml (½ cup) soy milk

60 ml (2 oz) olive oil

150 g (¾ cup) sugar

Dash of vanilla extract

50 g (¼ cup) soy yogurt

115 g (⅞ cup) self-rising flour

45 g (⅜ cup) cocoa powder

1 tsp baking powder

⅓ tsp baking soda

Pinch of salt

50 g (³⁄₁₀ cup) vegan chocolate chips

FROSTING
250 g (1¹⁄₁₀ cups) vegan stick butter, room temperature

300 g (1½ cups) powdered sugar

Dash of vanilla extract

FILLING AND TOPPING
150 g (5 oz) cherry jam

30 g (1 oz) grated vegan dark chocolate

250 g (1⅓ cups) pitted fresh cherries

Easy Chocolate Fondants

If there's one thing that you need to add to your list of things to bake this week, then it should be these Easy Chocolate Fondants. They taste like little pots of chocolate heaven, and I guarantee that you'll be surprised at how easy they are to make! Inside the soft, moist chocolate sponge cake is an oozing, rich molten filling.

Start by making the gooey ganache center. Melt the chocolate over a bain-marie and whisk in the cream. Pour this mixture into a container and place in the freezer to set for 1 to 2 hours.

When you're ready to make the fondants, preheat your oven to 355°F (180°C). Lightly grease four pudding molds with vegan butter and dust with a layer of cocoa powder.

To make the sponges, using a wooden spoon, cream together the olive oil and sugar until slightly pale. Pour in the warm water and milk and whisk together.

Sift the self-rising flour, cocoa powder and baking soda. Fold these into the wet ingredients along with the instant coffee and salt until you're left with a smooth, chocolaty batter.

Add a little of the mixture into the base of each of your pudding molds to fill about one-fourth of the way. Scoop out a little of your set chocolate filling and mold it into a rough ball. Place these into each of the pudding cups and cover with more of the batter to fill your molds three-fourths of the way to the top.

Bake the fondants for 15 minutes, then allow to cool for a couple of minutes. To serve, gently loosen the edges with a knife, place a plate on top and carefully flip to release the fondant. Garnish with fresh mint, and serve with fresh fruit or vegan ice cream if desired.

Yield: 4 fondants

FILLING
100 g (4 oz) vegan milk chocolate (if you would like a richer center, you can use a combination of plant-based milk and dark chocolate)

80 ml (3 oz) vegan cream

FONDANTS
Vegan butter, for greasing

40 ml (8 tsp) olive oil

130 g (⅔ cups) superfine or granulated sugar

100 ml (3 oz) warm water

100 ml (3 oz) nondairy milk (soy, almond or coconut work well)

145 g (1⅛ cups) self-rising flour

50 g (⅜ cup) high-quality cocoa powder, plus more for dusting

½ tsp baking soda

½ tsp instant coffee (can omit this if you would prefer)

Pinch of salt

TOPPING (OPTIONAL)
Fresh mint

Fresh fruit

Vegan ice cream

Loaf & Bundt Cakes

I decided to dedicate this chapter jointly to loaf and Bundt cakes, because as different as they are, they're both cakes that I opt for when looking for something easy yet showstopping. You can, of course, decorate them with frostings and toppings of your choosing, but their perfect simplicity also means they can be served just as they are! Both are also perfect when I know I'm going to be catering to a larger number of guests, as they provide a generous number of slices per cake and are also easy to serve and eat. Extravagant layer cakes with lashings of buttercream are delicious, but I can't deny they would be incredibly messy to eat with your hands!

As I mentioned, all these recipes can be served either as they are or with the accompanying frostings/glazes depending on your preferences. I'm always an advocate for getting creative in the kitchen and putting your own little spin on recipes, so feel free to experiment and find your favorite combination!

There's no denying that a Bundt cake makes for an utterly incredible and showstopping dessert, but they can pose their challenges. The big one being removing the cake from its pan. I've included some simple, step-by-step instructions to ensure that you're able to achieve the perfect Bundt every time. Follow them and you'll be just fine!

Passion Fruit & Yogurt Loaf Cake

This Passion Fruit & Yogurt Loaf Cake is what I crave whenever I fancy something fresh and fruity! It's bursting with vibrant tropical flavor and has the perfect moist sponge cake texture! This is an excellent pairing with an afternoon cup of tea or if you're after a dessert that can be easily enjoyed while you're on the go.

Preheat the oven to 355°F (180°C) and line an 8-inch (20-cm) loaf pan with parchment paper.

To make the vegan buttermilk alternative, add the apple cider vinegar to the soy milk, stir and let thicken for 5 minutes.

Start by adding the sugar and olive oil to a large mixing bowl and cream them together until pale and fluffy.

Whisk in the buttermilk, yogurt and vanilla, then sift the self-rising flour, baking powder and baking soda and fold these into the wet ingredients along with a pinch of salt. Stir in the fresh passion fruit and transfer the batter into the loaf pan.

Bake for 45 minutes, until cooked through. Check to see if your cake is ready by inserting a toothpick. If it comes out clean, the cake is cooked through.

Allow the cake to cool while you whip up the frosting.

Beat the butter until pale and fluffy, then gradually add the powdered sugar and vanilla while continuing to mix. Once the frosting is wonderfully thick and creamy, spread it over the top of the cake and top with fresh berries and some extra passion fruit and garnish with fresh mint.

Yield: 9–12 Servings

CAKE
15 ml (1 tbsp) apple cider vinegar

125 ml (½ cup) soy milk

155 g (¾ cup) golden superfine or granulated sugar

60 ml (2 oz) olive oil

100 g (½ cup) soy or almond yogurt

½ tsp vanilla bean paste

250 g (2 cups) self-rising flour

1¾ tsp baking powder

½ tsp baking soda

Pinch of salt

Filling from 1½ fresh passion fruit

FROSTING
200 g (⅞ cup) vegan stick butter, room temperature

250 g (1¼ cups) powdered sugar

½ tsp vanilla bean paste

TOPPINGS
200 g (1½ cups) fresh or frozen mixed berries

Filling from 2 fresh passion fruit

Fresh mint

Apple Crumble Loaf Cake

I would highly recommend making this recipe at any time of year, but its scents and flavors are that little bit more special during the autumn and winter months. It's the epitome of a cozy, comforting dessert and will have notes of baked apple and warming spices wafting through your kitchen as it bakes.

Preheat your oven to 355°F (180°C) and line an 8-inch (20-cm) loaf pan with parchment paper.

To make the vegan buttermilk alternative, add the apple cider vinegar to the soy milk, stir and let thicken for 5 minutes.

Beat the olive oil and sugar together, then stir in the buttermilk, vanilla and grated apple. Sift the self-rising flour, baking powder and baking soda. Add the dry ingredients into the wet mixture along with the cinnamon, mixed spice, ginger and a pinch of salt. Fold the wet and dry ingredients together to combine, then transfer to your loaf pan.

For the crumble mixture, combine the butter, sugar and plain flour together to form little crumble clusters and scatter these over your loaf. Bake for 40 minutes, until beautifully golden and crisp on top.

Remove from the oven and allow to cool on a cooling rack before topping with sliced apples and star anise and slicing into portions.

Yield: 10–12 Servings

CAKE
15 ml (1 tbsp) apple cider vinegar

250 ml (8 oz) soy milk

100 ml (4 oz) olive oil

160 g (¾ cup) golden superfine or granulated sugar

½ tsp vanilla paste

1 large apple, grated

250 g (2 cups) self-rising flour

2 tsp baking powder

⅓ tsp baking soda

1 tsp ground cinnamon

½ tsp mixed spice

¼ tsp ground ginger

Pinch of salt

CRUMBLE MIXTURE
14 g (1 tbsp) nondairy butter spread

24 g (2 tbsp) golden superfine or granulated sugar

16 g (2 tbsp) plain flour

TOPPING
Sliced apples

Star anise

Simple Chocolate-Chip Banana Loaf

This is my ultimate banana bread recipe and is something that has been made countless times in my household! It's deliciously sweet, fluffy, chocolaty and oh-so-easy to make! This recipe requires minimal equipment and effort and only a selection of simple ingredients. Whether you're a beginner or expert baker, a good banana bread recipe is an absolute must. It's perfect for any occasion and easy to slice for sharing or dessert on the go. I also love to freeze any leftovers and pop a slice in the toaster for a quick afternoon treat!

Preheat your oven to 355°F (180°C) and line an 8-inch (20-cm) loaf pan with parchment paper.

To make the vegan buttermilk alternative, add the apple cider vinegar to the soy milk, stir and let thicken for 5 minutes.

In a large mixing bowl, combine the olive oil and sugar and beat using a wooden spoon. Mash the bananas into a puree using the back of a fork (a potato masher is also a great hack for this) and stir them in.

Whisk in the buttermilk and vanilla, then sift in the self-rising flour and add the baking powder, baking soda, cinnamon, nutmeg and salt. Fold the wet and dry ingredients together to fully combine.

Stir in the chocolate and pour the mixture into your loaf pan. Bake for 50 to 55 minutes, until cooked through and golden on top, then allow to cool thoroughly.

This cake is delicious served as it is, but you can also add an extra special finishing touch with a simple icing sugar glaze and extra banana slices. To make the glaze, mix the powdered sugar and nondairy milk together and drizzle this over the top of the cake.

Yield: 9–12 Servings

CAKE

15 ml (1 tbsp) apple cider vinegar

125 ml (½ cup) soy milk

60 ml (2 oz) olive oil (or other neutral vegetable oil)

120 g (⅝ cup) golden superfine or granulated sugar

200 g (1 cup) ripe bananas

½ tsp vanilla paste or extract

250 g (2 cups) self-rising flour

5 g (2 tsp) baking powder

⅓ tsp baking soda

1 tsp ground cinnamon

Pinch of ground nutmeg

Pinch of salt

80 g (3 oz) chopped vegan dark chocolate or chocolate chips

GLAZE

120 g (1 cup) powdered sugar

30–60 g (2–4 tbsp) nondairy milk

TOPPING

Banana slices

Blueberry & Vanilla Pound Cake

Wonderfully simple and yet still incredibly delicious, this Blueberry & Vanilla Pound Cake is the perfect dessert for a mid-afternoon snack to accompany a cup of tea. It can be enjoyed as it is or topped with an array of your favorite spreads. While being a sweet treat, this recipe is also understated enough to make enjoying a slice of cake for breakfast acceptable.

(180°C) and line a standard-sized loaf pan with parchment paper.

To make the vegan buttermilk alternative, add the apple cider vinegar to the soy milk, stir and let thicken for 5 minutes.

In a mixing bowl, use a wooden spoon to cream the sugar and olive oil together. Mix through the buttermilk, yogurt and vanilla to fully combine, then sift 250 grams (2 cups) of the self-rising flour, baking powder and baking soda into the bowl.

Fold the wet and dry ingredients together to create a smooth and airy batter. Toss the blueberries in the remaining teaspoon of flour to coat, then carefully stir these into your cake mixture.

Transfer the batter to the loaf pan and bake for 40 minutes, until beautifully risen and light golden in color.

While your loaf is cooling, mix the powdered sugar and milk to create a pourable glaze. Drizzle this over your loaf and garnish with fresh blueberries and mint leaves.

Yield: 9–12 Servings

CAKE
15 ml (1 tbsp) apple cider vinegar

120 ml (½ cup) soy milk

20 g (⅛ cup) superfine or granulated sugar

90 ml (6 tbsp) olive oil

100 g (½ cup) soy yogurt

½ tsp vanilla bean paste

250 g (2 cups) plus 1 tsp self-rising flour, divided

1½ tsp baking powder

⅓ tsp baking soda

150 g (¾ cup) fresh or frozen blueberries

GLAZE
150 g (¾ cup) powdered sugar

15–30 ml (1–2 tbsp) nondairy milk or water

TOPPINGS
200 g (1 cup) fresh blueberries

Fresh mint leaves

Preheat the oven to 355°F

Blackberry & Lemon Loaf Cake

For me, this Blackberry & Lemon Loaf Cake screams summer teatime dessert! I can just picture it as the perfect addition to a glorious alfresco afternoon table or picnic spread. It's deceivingly simple to make and always has the perfect, moist sponge cake texture! The cake itself is light and fluffy, with gloriously juicy blackberries studded throughout so that each mouthful contains a little burst of those delicious, sweet juices! It's another easy, one-bowl recipe, perfect if you don't want to spend ages in the kitchen and don't want to compromise on taste. This is one of my go-to recipes for spring and summertime whenever I'm tasked with bringing dessert, which as I'm sure you've guessed, is always!

Preheat your oven to 355°F (180°C) and prepare a standard-sized loaf pan by lining it with parchment paper.

To make the vegan buttermilk alternative, add 15 milliliters (1 tablespoon) of lemon juice to the soy milk, stir and let thicken for 5 minutes.

In a mixing bowl, rub the lemon zest together with the sugar using your fingers. Pour in the olive oil and cream the sugar and oil using a wooden spoon.

Whisk through the buttermilk, yogurt and remaining 30 milliliters (2 tablespoons) of lemon juice to combine. Sift 200 grams (1⅝ cups) of the self-rising flour, baking powder and baking soda and fold the wet and dry ingredients together.

Once you're left with a smooth batter, toss the blackberries in the 8 grams (1 tablespoon) of flour, and carefully stir them into the cake batter.

Transfer the mixture to your loaf pan and bake for 40 minutes. Remove the loaf from the oven and let cool completely.

To make the glaze, mix the sugar and water until it is smooth and pourable. Drizzle this over your loaf and decorate with fresh berries.

Yield: 9-12 Servings

CAKE
45 ml (3 tbsp) lemon juice, divided

125 ml (½ cup) soy milk

Zest from 2 lemons

150 g (¾ cup) golden superfine or granulated sugar

65 ml (2 oz) olive oil

45 g (¼ cup) soy yogurt

200 g (1⅝ cups) plus 8 g (1 tbsp) self-rising flour, divided

5 g (2 tsp) baking powder

⅓ tsp baking soda

150 g (1 cup) fresh blackberries

GLAZE
200 g (1½ cups) powdered sugar

30–60 ml (2–4 tbsp) water or nondairy milk

TOPPINGS
Fresh blackberries

Fresh strawberries

Marbled Strawberry Loaf Cake

After experimenting with other fresh strawberry recipes, I couldn't resist testing out a loaf cake. This cake is made with heaps of fresh strawberries, which not only keep the sponge wonderfully moist but also add the most incredible, authentic sweet flavor. This is one of my go-to recipes to bake when I'm hosting a lunch, picnic or tea with friends!

Preheat your oven to 355°F (180°C) and line a standard-sized loaf pan with parchment paper.

To make the vegan buttermilk alternative, add the apple cider vinegar to the soy milk, stir and let thicken for 5 minutes.

Put the berries in a food processor, then blitz into a smooth puree. You don't need to strain this, but you can if you would prefer. In a large mixing bowl, combine the sugar and olive oil and cream until pale in color.

Pour in the buttermilk and vanilla, then gently fold the flour, lime zest, baking powder, baking soda and salt. Finally, stir in the strawberry puree, a few drops of pink food coloring and the freeze-dried berries (these provide a great pop of additional flavor!).

Take approximately one-third of the cake batter, add a few extra drops of food coloring and mix.

Pour the cake mixture into the loaf pan, add the darker mixture on top and carefully swirl these together using a skewer or toothpick. Bake for 45 to 50 minutes. Once cooked, allow your cake to cool slightly in the pan, then transfer to wire rack to finish cooling.

Prepare the icing by mixing the powdered sugar gradually with a little water or milk until you're left with a spreadable (but not too runny) consistency. Spread the icing over the cooled cake and top with the fresh berries!

Yield: 9-12 Servings

CAKE
15 ml (1 tbsp) apple cider vinegar

125 ml (½ cup) soy milk

400 g (3¼ cups) fresh sliced strawberries

300 g (1 cup) superfine or granulated sugar

118 ml (4 oz) olive oil

Dash of vanilla extract

300 g (2⅖ cups) plain flour

Zest from 2 limes

5 g (2 tsp) baking powder

½ tsp baking soda

Pinch of salt

Vegan-friendly pink food coloring or beetroot powder

1–2 g (1–2 tbsp) freeze-dried berries

GLAZE
240 g (1¼ cups) powdered sugar

30–60 ml (2–4 tbsp) water or nondairy milk

TOPPING
Fresh sliced strawberries, rasberries and pomegranate seeds

Carrot Cake Loaf

This Carrot Cake Loaf contains several different fruits and vegetables, so technically, I'm thinking this makes it somewhat acceptable to serve as a sweet breakfast. This lightly spiced loaf cake is wonderfully moist, sweet and couldn't be simpler to make!

Preheat your oven to 355°F (180°C) and prepare your standard-sized loaf pan by lining it with parchment paper.

To make the vegan buttermilk alternative, add the lemon juice to the soy milk, stir and let thicken for 5 minutes.

In a large mixing bowl, cream together the sugar and olive oil. Add the mashed banana, grated apple and carrot, then pour in the buttermilk and whisk everything to combine.

Sift the flour, baking powder and baking soda to remove any lumps. Fold these into the wet ingredients along with the mixed spice, cinnamon, nutmeg, orange zest and a pinch of salt.

Pour the mixture into the loaf pan and bake for 1 hour. Remove once golden and cooked through, then allow to cool completely.

To make the frosting, start by beating the butter and cream cheese together using an electric hand mixer on low to medium speed. Mix for about 2 minutes, until pale and fluffy. Gradually add the sugar while continuing to whisk to fully combine.

To decorate, spread or pipe the cream cheese frosting over the top of the cake and garnish with the fresh berries and orange zest.

Yield: 9-12 Servings

CAKE
15 ml (1 tbsp) lemon juice

150 ml (5 oz) soy milk

130 g (⅔ cup) sugar

65 ml (2 oz) olive oil

80 g (⅓ cup) ripe banana, mashed

80 g (⅓ cup) grated apple

80 g (⅓ cup) grated carrot

250 g (2 cups) plain flour

5 g (2 tsp) baking powder

½ tsp baking soda

⅓ tsp mixed spice

1 tsp ground cinnamon

Pinch of nutmeg

Zest from 1 orange

Pinch of salt

CREAM CHEESE FROSTING
100 g (½ cup) vegan stick butter, room temperature

100 g (½ cup) vegan cream cheese

250 g (1¼ cups) powdered sugar

TOPPING
150 g (1 cup) fresh berries

2 tbsp orange zest

Chocolate Bundt Cake with Rich Chocolate Glaze

A Bundt cake is one of those desserts that doesn't require layers of frosting or fancy decoration; they're exceptionally impressive by themselves and the perfect celebration cake for any event. This rich Chocolate Bundt Cake is indulgently moist, divinely laden with chocolate and finished with an elegant dark chocolate glaze.

Preheat your oven to 355°F (180°C). Grease the inside of a 9.6-inch (24.5-cm) Bundt pan with vegan butter or nondairy spread, ensuring all the areas are coated. Then lightly dust with cocoa powder and tip out any excess.

To make the vegan buttermilk alternative, add the apple cider vinegar to the nondairy milk, stir and let thicken for 5 minutes.

In a large mixing bowl, beat together the sugar and olive oil until slightly pale and fluffy. Pour in the buttermilk, yogurt and coffee, then whisk them together.

Sift the cocoa powder, flour, baking powder, baking soda and a pinch of salt. Carefully fold the dry and wet ingredients together until you're left with a completely smooth batter.

Pour this into your Bundt pan, ensuring that the mixture is evenly spread around the pan. Bake for 50 to 55 minutes, until completely cooked through. Check to see if your cake is ready by inserting a toothpick. If it comes out clean, the cakes are cooked through. Leave the cake to completely cool in the pan.

Meanwhile, for the glaze, place the chocolate in a heatproof bowl over a saucepan of gently boiling water. Allow it to melt and then whisk in the cream and maple syrup. You're aiming for a glossy, pourable consistency.

Once cooled, carefully flip the cake onto a serving plate and the pan should easily lift away. If this doesn't happen, you can use a knife to loosen around the edges very carefully.

Pour the chocolate glaze over the cake and allow this to drizzle down the outer edges of the cake. To serve, I love to fill the center of the cake with heaps of glorious fresh fruit!

Yield: 12-16 Servings

BUNDT CAKE

15 ml (1 tbsp) apple cider vinegar

130 ml (4 oz) nondairy milk

400 g (2 cups) superfine or granulated sugar

100 ml (4 oz) olive oil

100 g (½ cup) soy, almond or coconut yogurt

100 ml (½ cup) strong-brewed coffee or espresso

67 g (½ cup) cocoa powder, plus more for dusting

400 g (3¼ cups) self-rising flour

5 g (2 tsp) baking powder

½ tsp baking soda

Pinch of sea salt

CHOCOLATE GLAZE

100 g (4 oz) vegan dark chocolate

125 ml (4 oz) vegan cream

15–30 ml (1–2 tbsp) maple syrup (or to taste)

TOPPING

500 g (3 cups) fresh mixed berries

Marbled Gingerbread Bundt Cake

While I consider it to be acceptable to make this cake any time of year, it's undoubtedly the perfect addition to your Christmas dessert menu! If you're hosting a Christmas feast or have been tasked with bringing a dessert, then look no further than this recipe!

Preheat your oven to 355°F (180°C). To prep your Bundt pan, grease all the inner surface area with vegan butter or spread and lightly dust this with flour. This will prevent your cake from sticking and allow for easy removal.

To make the vegan buttermilk alternative for both cakes, in separate bowls, mix one portion each of lemon juice into one portion each of the soy milk, stir and let thicken for 5 minutes.

First make the gingerbread cake batter. In a large mixing bowl, cream the sugar and olive oil together until slightly pale in color. Whisk in one portion of the buttermilk.

Sift the self-rising flour, baking powder and baking soda into the bowl, then add the mixed spice, ginger, cinnamon, nutmeg and a pinch of salt. Fold the wet and dry ingredients together to fully combine.

For the chocolate cake, beat the olive oil and sugar together, then whisk in the second portion of buttermilk. Sift in the cocoa powder, self-rising flour, baking powder and baking soda. Then add the ground cinnamon and a good pinch of salt. Fold the wet and dry ingredients together to combine fully.

Yield: 12–16 Servings

GINGERBREAD SPONGE
15 ml (1 tbsp) lemon juice

240 ml (8 oz) soy milk

260 g (1⅓ cups) sugar

100 ml (4 oz) olive oil

300 g (2⅖ cups) self-rising flour, plus more for dusting

5 g (2 tsp) baking powder

⅓ tsp baking soda

1 tsp mixed spice

⅓ tsp ground ginger

1 tsp ground cinnamon

Pinch of nutmeg

Pinch of salt

CHOCOLATE SPONGE
15 ml (1 tbsp) lemon juice

180 ml (6 oz) soy milk

90 ml (6 tbsp) olive oil

200 g (1 cup) sugar

40 g (⅜ cup) high-quality cocoa powder

200 g (1⅝ cups) self-rising flour

5 g (2 tsp) baking powder

⅓ tsp baking soda

1 tsp ground cinnamon

Pinch of salt

Fill your Bundt pan starting with a layer of gingerbread cake batter in the base and top with a few heaping spoonfuls of the chocolate mixture. Repeat this process until all the batter is used up, then bake for 55 to 60 minutes. Check to see if your cake is ready by inserting a toothpick. If it comes out clean, the cake is cooked through.

Leave your Bundt cake to cool in the pan. To remove the cake, gently loosen the edges with a knife, then place your serving plate on top of the cake. Carefully flip this over and lift the pan away.

This cake can be served as it is or finished with a cinnamon glaze.

To make the cinnamon glaze, mix together the powdered sugar, milk and cinnamon until smooth. Drizzle this over the entire cake, allowing it to flow gloriously over the outer edges.

CINNAMON GLAZE

200 g (1⅔ cup) powdered sugar

30 to 60 ml (2-4 tbsp) nondairy milk

Pinch of ground cinnamon

Celebration & Occasion Cakes

This chapter is dedicated to those special cakes designed to bring an extra touch of deliciousness to your celebrations. If you're looking to cater to vegan guests or maybe showcase to your friends just how delicious plant-based desserts can be, these will do just that! In this section, you'll find a selection of my favorite showstopping cakes, with something to suit every occasion and season.

Whether it be Christmas, birthdays or a simple dinner with friends, food plays such an important role in our celebrations and is something we're able to experience and enjoy together. I love being able to make something that I know my friends and family are going to love. Plus, I feel like having a homemade cake is always a really special, thoughtful addition to a celebration feast!

While they require slightly more time and preparation, as some of these cakes are rather extravagant, I can assure you that they're worth it! I'm always a sucker for anything spiced and autumnal, so the Pumpkin-Spiced Layer Cake (page 149) and Caramel Apple Showstopper (page 141) are my personal favorites for the cooler months. If you're after an all-around occasion cake, then I will always recommend my Ombré Raspberry Layer Cake (page 139). This is the perfect balance of fresh yet indulgent and always makes for a stunning centerpiece! If it's something chocolate-laden that you're after, don't worry because there's plenty of that, too!

Ombré Raspberry Layer Cake

I feel like I'm going to find myself saying this about quite a few recipes, but this is one of my absolute favorite showstopper cakes! It's an utterly stunning centerpiece for a celebration table spread, with a gorgeous balance of sweet and fruity flavors.

If you're after something decadent, extravagant but perhaps a little lighter and fresher than a rich chocolate cake, then this ombré raspberry layer cake is for you! The cake consists of three layers of fluffy, lemon-infused sponge cake, paired with vibrant layers of raspberry jam and juicy fresh raspberries studded throughout. Lemon and raspberry is one of my favorite fruity flavor combinations, as the bright citrus really compliments the berries. The ombré buttercream coating gives the cake that wow factor, whilst still being surprisingly easy to create! This is the perfect recipe if you're looking to impress and I can guarantee, vegan or not, your guests will love this!

Preheat your oven to 355°F (180°C) and line three 6½-inch (17-cm) loose-bottom cake pans with parchment paper.

To make the vegan buttermilk alternative, add the lemon juice to the soy milk, stir and let thicken for 5 minutes.

In a large mixing bowl, cream the olive oil, sugar and lemon zest together using a wooden spoon. This can also be done using a stand mixer if you prefer.

Whisk in the buttermilk and vanilla to combine. Sift the self-rising flour, baking powder and baking soda into the bowl and gently fold these into the wet ingredients. Once the batter is nice and smooth, divide this evenly among the cake pans.

Bake for 30 to 35 minutes, until beautifully risen and golden, then remove from the oven and allow to cool. After 5 minutes, remove the cake pans carefully and transfer to a wire rack to finish cooling.

(continued)

Yield: 10-12 Servings

CAKE

30 ml (2 tbsp) fresh lemon juice

300 ml (10 oz) soy or almond milk

135 ml (4 oz) olive oil

300 g (1½ cups) superfine or granulated sugar

Zest from 2 lemons

½ tsp vanilla extract or paste

405 g (3¼ cups) self-rising flour

8 g (3 tsp) baking powder

½ tsp baking soda

Ombré Raspberry Layer Cake (Continued)

For the ombré frosting, start by adding the butter to a stand mixer or an electric hand whisk and beat until pale and fluffy. This should take a few minutes.

Gradually add the powdered sugar and lemon zest while mixing until everything is incorporated. Mix for a few minutes more so that you're left with a super creamy consistency.

Divide the buttercream among three bowls and add a few drops of food coloring to one of the bowls and a few more to the second to create a darker pink. You should be left with white, pale pink and dark pink frostings.

Once the cake has cooled, spread a little of the dark pink buttercream onto one of the cake layers and top with some of the jam and fresh raspberries. Sandwich the second layer on top and repeat this using the paler shade of frosting. Place the final layer on top and frost with the white frosting.

To create the ombré effect, spread your layers of frosting onto the outside of the cake, starting with the dark on the bottom. Use a cake scraper to smooth and seamlessly blend the colors. I like to use a spoon or small palette knife to create a ribbed effect.

Top with more of the fresh raspberries and a handful of mint leaves before serving.

FROSTING

350 g (1½ cups) vegan stick butter, room temperature

450 g (2¼ cups) powdered sugar

Zest from 1 lemon

A few drops of vegan pink food coloring

FILLING

150 g (5 oz) raspberry jam

250 g (1½ cups) fresh raspberries

Zest from 1 lemon

TOPPINGS

200 g (1½ cups) fresh raspberries

Handful fresh mint leaves

Caramel Apple Showstopper Cake

Of all the cakes I've made, it's almost impossible to choose just one favorite. However, if I had to pick an ultimate knockout recipe, then I think it would have to be this Caramel Apple Showstopper Cake. I make this recipe for an autumn event every year without fail, and I don't think I will ever get bored of it! There are four incredible layers of soft apple sponge cake, a creamy cinnamon spiced buttercream, homemade caramel drizzle and crunchy caramel coated apples. This cake is seriously indulgent, and I can't wait for you to try it!

Preheat your oven to 355°F (180°C) and line four 7-inch (18-cm) loose-bottom cake pans with parchment paper.

To make the vegan buttermilk alternative, add the apple cider vinegar to the soy milk, stir and let thicken for 5 minutes.

In a large mixing bowl, add the olive oil, butter, brown sugar and superfine sugar. Either by hand or using an electric whisk, beat these well until pale and fluffy. This should only take 1 to 2 minutes. Using a wooden spoon, stir in the buttermilk, grated apple and yogurt to combine.

Sift the self-rising flour, baking powder and baking soda and add these into the bowl along with a pinch of salt, the vanilla, cinnamon and nutmeg. Fold the wet and dry ingredients well to bring everything together into a smooth batter.

Divide the batter evenly among the cake pans and bake for 30 to 32 minutes, then remove from the oven and let cool completely.

(continued)

Yield: 12 Servings

CAKE

15 ml (1 tbsp) apple cider vinegar

270 ml (9 oz) soy milk

100 ml (4 oz) olive oil

80 g (¼ cup) vegan stick butter, room temperature

200 g (1 cup) soft brown sugar

200 g (1 cup) superfine or granulated sugar

240 g (2 cups) grated apple

185 g (⅗ cup) soy yogurt

540 g (4⅓ cups) self-rising flour

10 g (4 tsp) baking powder

¾ tsp baking soda

Pinch of salt

1 tsp vanilla paste

6 g (2 tsp) ground cinnamon

Pinch of nutmeg

Caramel Apple Showstopper Cake (Continued)

Meanwhile, to make the caramel, add the sugar, salt and coconut milk to a saucepan and bring to a low boil for about 15 minutes, stirring continuously.

Once you're left with a golden, rich caramel color, remove from the heat and allow this to cool and thicken for 5 to 10 minutes. You want the caramel to be slightly warm and still runny when you dip the apples.

Dip each of the apples into the caramel and place them onto a lined baking sheet to allow them to set. I love to add apple-tree branches as "skewers" here also!

Start making the frosting by beating the butter until pale and fluffy. I use an electric hand whisk, but you can also use a stand mixer for this. Start adding the powdered sugar and cinnamon while mixing and continue until everything is fully incorporated.

Spread a layer of frosting onto the first sponge cake and carefully place a second sponge on top. Repeat this process for the other two. Coat the whole cake in a thin layer of frosting using the remaining icing to create a naked frosting effect. Spread a generous layer of the caramel sauce on top, allowing this to create a drip effect over the sides. Refrigerate the cake for 5 to 10 minutes to help the caramel set slightly and not run into the frosting.

Finish by topping with the caramel apples and other decorations of choice. I love adding some crushed biscuit crumbs and cinnamon sugar.

CARAMEL
150 g (¾ cup) light brown sugar

Generous pinch of salt

300 ml (10 oz) canned coconut milk

3 apples (I use Braeburn or pink lady apples)

FROSTING
300 g (1⅓ cups) vegan stick butter, room temperature

400 g (2 cups) powdered sugar

¾ tsp ground cinnamon

TOPPING
Crushed biscuits

Cinnamon sugar

Double Chocolate Birthday Cake

When it comes to birthday cakes, I feel like you can seldom go wrong with something decadent and chocolaty—and if you agree, then this cake is a winner! Plus, if you're looking for something to impress your non-vegan guests, then I couldn't think of a better place to start. With a moist, rich sponge cake and lashings of creamy frosting heaven, no one will ever guess this is vegan!

Preheat your oven to 355°F (180°C) and line three 6½-inch (17-cm) cake pans with parchment paper.

To make the vegan buttermilk alternative, add the apple cider vinegar to the soy milk, stir and let thicken for 5 minutes.

In a large mixing bowl, use a wooden spoon to beat together the sugar and olive oil until slightly pale and fluffy. Whisk through the buttermilk and yogurt to fully combine.

Sift the self-rising flour, cocoa powder, baking powder, baking soda, then add the dry ingredients to the mixing bowl. Fold both the wet and dry ingredients together until you're left with a smooth batter.

Divide the mixture among the lined cake pans and bake for 25 to 27 minutes. When these are nicely risen and slightly crisp on top, remove them from the oven and allow to cool on a wire rack.

Meanwhile, to make the frosting, beat the butter until pale and fluffy using an electric hand whisk or stand mixer.

Gradually add the cocoa powder and powdered sugar while continuing to mix until everything is fully incorporated.

Once the cakes have cooled completely, spread a generous layer of frosting onto one of the cake layers, then carefully add the second on top. Repeat this with the third layer, then take the remaining frosting (reserving a small amount for the piping on top) and spread this over the cake to coat.

Use an offset spatula to evenly coat the cake in a buttercream layer, then take a cake scraper to remove any excess and create a smooth finish.

Add the remaining frosting to a piping bag with a star-tip nozzle and add decorative swirls to the top of the cake. Scatter rainbow sprinkles on top and serve.

Yield: 8–10 Servings

CAKE

15 ml (1 tbsp) apple cider vinegar

150 ml (5 oz) soy milk

160 g (¾ cup) superfine or granulated sugar

85 ml (3 oz) olive oil

100 g (½ cup) soy yogurt

200 g (1⅝ cups) self-rising flour

30 g (¼ cup) high-quality cocoa powder

5 g (2 tsp) baking powder

⅓ tsp baking soda

Pinch of salt

FROSTING

200 g (⅞ cup) vegan stick butter, room temperature

40 g (⅜ cup) high-quality cocoa powder

250 g (1 ¼ cups) powdered sugar

Rainbow sprinkles for decoration

Easter Nest Cake

This vegan Easter Nest Cake is the perfect, cute seasonal treat for your Easter celebrations! There are layers of lightly spiced sponge cake, subtly flavored with sweet orange zest. These are then sandwiched together with a creamy vanilla frosting and vibrant layer of berry jam. My favorite part, the speckled egg frosting, just makes this cake look so festive and just like a giant speckled easter egg! It's so simple to make and getting a little mouthful of dark chocolate in each bite of vanilla frosting just makes it even more delicious!

Preheat your oven to 355°F (180°C) and line two 6½-inch (17-cm) loose-bottom cake pans with parchment paper.

To make the vegan buttermilk alternative, add the lemon juice to the soy milk, stir and let thicken for 5 minutes.

In a large mixing bowl, rub the sugar, lemon zest and orange zest together using your fingers to infuse the citrus flavor. Use a wooden spoon to cream this together with the olive oil until pale and fluffy.

Whisk in the buttermilk and vanilla, then sift the self-rising flour, cinnamon, nutmeg, baking powder and baking soda. Fold the dry ingredients into the wet mixture until your batter is completely smooth.

Transfer the cake batter into your lined cake pans and bake for approximately 35 minutes, until risen and golden. Remove the pans from the oven and allow them to cool completely on a wire rack.

(continued)

Yield: 8–10 servings

CAKE

15 ml (1 tbsp) lemon juice

200 ml (7 oz) soy milk

240 g (1¼ cup) superfine or granulated sugar

Zest from 1 lemon

Zest from 1 orange

100 ml (4 oz) olive oil

Dash of vanilla extract

270 g (2⅛ cups) self-rising flour

1 tsp ground cinnamon

Pinch of nutmeg

5 g (2 tsp) baking powder

⅓ tsp baking soda

Easter Nest Cake (Continued)

For the speckled frosting, begin by creaming the butter until pale and fluffy. You can do this using an electric hand whisk or stand mixer on low to medium speed. Gradually add the sugar and mix until super smooth and creamy. Mix in a few drops of the food coloring to create a pale pink color.

Finely chop the dark chocolate, then fold it into the frosting to create the speckled-egg effect.

Once your cakes have cooled, it's time to assemble. Spread a generous layer of frosting onto one of the layers and top with the berry jam. Carefully place the second layer on top, then spread an even layer of the remaining frosting over the entire cake. Smooth this out and scrape off any excess using a palette knife and cake scraper.

Top with the mini chocolate eggs to decorate and serve.

FROSTING

270 g (1¼ cups) vegan stick butter, room temperature

350 g (1¾ cups) powdered sugar

Vegan-friendly pink food coloring or beetroot powder

50 g (2 oz) vegan dark or milk chocolate

FILLING

100 g (6⅔ tbsp) raspberry jam

TOPPING

80 g (2 oz) vegan mini chocolate eggs

Pumpkin-Spiced Layer Cake

If you're a pumpkin spice fan, then you're going to ADORE this layer cake recipe! I don't know about you, but as soon as September first rolls around, I'm headed straight to Starbucks to secure a heavenly cup of creamy spiced goodness! This cake is like a warming autumnal drink in dessert form with an ultra-soft pumpkin-spiced sponge—made using pumpkin puree! The cakes are then layered with a glorious plant-based cream cheese buttercream frosting, complete with sweet notes of cinnamon. If that wasn't already enough indulgence for you, this recipe also calls for browned butter, which of course just makes everything more delicious! This adds notes of rich nuttiness to the sponges. You're simply going to be obsessed!

Preheat the oven to 355°F (180°C). Line two 6½-inch (17-cm) loose-bottom cake pans with parchment paper.

To make the vegan buttermilk alternative, add the apple cider vinegar to the soy milk, stir and let thicken for 5 minutes.

To make the browned butter, melt the butter in a small saucepan on medium heat, whisking as it cooks. The butter should begin to foam and turn golden brown in color. Monitor it closely to prevent burning and remove it from the heat once it's golden brown and releasing an incredible nutty scent!

In a mixing bowl, combine the browned butter, sugar and olive oil, then mix well to combine using a wooden spoon.

Stir in the buttermilk, vanilla and canned pumpkin. Then sift the flour, baking powder and baking soda and fold these into the wet ingredients along with the cinnamon, mixed spice, cloves, ginger, nutmeg and salt.

Transfer your batter to the cake pans and bake for 30 to 35 minutes. Remove the cakes from the oven and allow them to cool on a wire rack.

(continued)

Yield: 8-10 Servings

CAKE

15 ml (1 tbsp) apple cider vinegar

170 ml (6 oz) soy milk

30 g (2 tbsp) vegan butter

180 g (⅞ cups) superfine or granulated sugar

50 ml (2 oz) olive oil

½ tsp vanilla bean paste

55 g (¼ cup) canned pumpkin

250 g (2 cups) self-rising flour

5 g (2 tsp) baking powder

⅓ tsp baking soda

1 tsp ground cinnamon

½ tsp mixed spice

¼ tsp ground cloves

¼ tsp ground ginger

Pinch of nutmeg

Pinch of salt

Pumpkin-Spiced Layer Cake (Continued)

While the cakes are cooling, you can prepare the spiced frosting! Start by beating the butter and cream cheese using an electric hand whisk or stand mixer on low to medium speed. Gradually add the powdered sugar, cinnamon and a pinch of nutmeg and continue mixing until all the sugar is fully incorporated.

Spread frosting over one of the cake layers, then sandwich the second on top. Coat the top of the cake with the remaining frosting using a cake scraper and palette knife to achieve a smooth finish. If desired, reserve enough of the frosting to fill a piping bag and add little swirls on top of the cake to finish!

I love to add cinnamon sticks, little chocolate pumpkins and star anise onto each of the frosting swirls to decorate!

FROSTING

200 g (⅞ cup) vegan stick butter, room temperature

100 g (½ cup) vegan cream cheese

400 g (2 cups) powdered sugar

1 tsp ground cinnamon

Pinch of nutmeg

TOPPINGS

Cinnamon sticks

Halloween chocolates (I use pumpkins)

Star anise

Bonfire Brownie Layer Cake

The best way for me to describe this Bonfire Brownie Layer Cake is to say that it's like a more indulgent, decadent version of my S'mores layer cake (page 60), with a little extra sparkle! There's even more caramel, extra chocolate, warming spices and these incredible homemade candy shards! This is the ultimate showstopper dessert to make for bonfire season and is guaranteed to be the star of the dinner table at any event! The layers of fudge brownie cake are sandwiched together with a delicious chocolate frosting, with a glorious chocolate drizzle gliding over the edges. I've used both brown sugar and superfine sugar for this chocolate cake, as I find this combination helps to create an even fudgier texture with a beautiful caramel hue.

Preheat your oven to 355°F (180°C) and line two 6½-inch (17-cm) loose-bottom cake pans with parchment paper.

To make the vegan buttermilk alternative, add the apple cider vinegar to the soy milk, stir and let thicken for 5 minutes.

Add the brown sugar, olive oil and superfine sugar to a large mixing bowl and cream together using a wooden spoon. Pour in the buttermilk and stir to combine.

Into this, fold the self-rising flour, oat flour, cocoa powder, vanilla bean powder, cinnamon, ginger, baking powder, baking soda and salt. Once you're left with a smooth, chocolaty batter, divide it between the two pans and bake for 30 to 32 minutes. Remove the cakes from the oven and allow them to cool.

(continued)

Yield: 8–10 Servings

CAKE

15 ml (1 tbsp) apple cider vinegar

200 ml (7 oz) soy or almond milk

40 g (¼ cup) soft brown sugar

85 ml (3 oz) olive oil

160 g (¾ cup) golden superfine or granulated sugar

150 g (1¼ cups) self-rising flour

90 g (1 cup) oat flour

35 g (⅓ cup) high-quality cocoa powder

½ tsp vanilla bean powder

1 tsp ground cinnamon

⅓ tsp ground ginger

1½ tsp baking powder

½ tsp baking soda

Pinch of salt

Bonfire Brownie Layer Cake (Continued)

Meanwhile, for the frosting, beat the butter using an electric whisk or stand mixer until pale and fluffy. Continue to mix while gradually incorporating the powdered sugar and beat for a further few minutes.

Gently melt the chocolate and fold half of it through the frosting. The remaining chocolate will be used to create the chocolate drip effect.

Start frosting the cake by spreading an even layer of buttercream over one of the sponges and topping with a sprinkling of the crushed biscuits. Sandwich the second layer on top and use the remaining frosting to coat the cake. Refrigerate for 10 minutes.

For the showstopping caramel shards, place the sugar and water into a saucepan over medium-low heat to allow the sugar to dissolve. Don't stir the sugar yet—you can swirl the pan to help dissolve the sugar if necessary. Once the sugar has dissolved, increase the heat to medium-high and leave the mixture to bubble for around 10 minutes, until golden.

Pour the sugar onto a parchment-lined tray and sprinkle generously with some sea salt flakes. Allow it to cool for 20 to 30 minutes. Check that the caramel has cooled and solidified, then break into shards. This is the fun part!

Use the remaining chocolate to drip around the sides of your cake, then garnish with the remaining biscuit crumbs, the caramel shards and toasted marshmallows.

If you're serving this for a Bonfire night party or special occasion, these party cake sparklers are an excellent way to add that show-stopping effect that will definitely impress your guests!

FROSTING

250 g (¾ cup) vegan stick butter, room temperature

300 g (1½ cups) powdered sugar

150 g (6 oz) vegan dark chocolate

CARAMEL SHARDS

220 g (1⅛ cups) superfine or granulated sugar

45–60 ml (3–4 tbsp) water

Pinch of sea salt flakes

TOPPINGS

50 g (½ cup) vegan biscuits, crushed (I use Lotus Biscoff®), divided

Handful vegan marshmallows, toasted

Spiced-Orange Christmas Layer Cake

This cake is kind of like my Christmas pudding substitute for people who like fruit and spices but aren't quite fans of the classic Christmas pudding! These sponge cake layers are pillowy soft, perfectly moist and flavored with a divine combination of sweet cinnamon, ginger and mixed spice. The warming spices pair beautifully with the subtle hues of orange flavor and instantly transport me to a festive paradise with each bite! I love serving this cake on Christmas Eve to accompany a gingerbread-spiced hot chocolate while watching back-to-back Christmas movies—pure perfection!

Preheat the oven to 355°F (180°C) and line two 6½-inch (17-cm) loose-bottom cake pans with parchment paper.

To make the vegan buttermilk alternative, add the apple cider vinegar to the soy milk, stir and let thicken for 5 minutes.

In a large mixing bowl, cream together the sugar and olive oil using a wooden spoon. Once fully combined, whisk in the buttermilk, then fold in the self-rising flour, orange zest, cinnamon, pumpkin pie spice, ginger, baking powder and baking soda to fully combine.

Stir in the mixed fruit, then divide the mixture between both cake pans and bake for approximately 35 minutes. When cooked through, transfer to a wire rack to cool completely.

(continued)

Yield: 8-10 Servings

CAKE

15 ml (1 tbsp) apple cider vinegar

200 ml (7 oz) soy milk

180 g (⅞ cup) golden superfine or granulated sugar

80 ml (3 oz) olive oil or other neutral vegetable oil

230 g (1⅞ cups) self-rising flour

Zest from 1 orange

1 tsp ground cinnamon

½ tsp pumpkin pie spice

¼ tsp ground ginger

5 g (2 tsp) baking powder

⅓ tsp baking soda

40 g (¼ cup) dried mixed fruit (raisins, golden raisins and currants)

Spiced-Orange Christmas Layer Cake (Continued)

To make the frosting, beat the butter for 2 to 3 minutes, until pale and fluffy. Add the cinnamon and vanilla, then gradually incorporate the powdered sugar and continue to mix until everything is fully combined and really creamy!

To assemble the cake, spread frosting onto the first cake layer using a palette knife, then carefully place the second on top. Spread frosting over the entire outside of the cake and smooth this over using a cake scraper and palette knife to create an even finish.

Use any remaining frosting to pipe decorative swirls on top of your cake. I love to garnish this with vegan caramel sauce, mini gingerbread men and red currants for a festive look. As always, you can get creative and add whatever you'd like.

FROSTING

250 g (1¹⁄₁₀) vegan stick butter

½ tsp ground cinnamon

½ tsp vanilla bean paste

300 g (1½ cups) powdered sugar

TOPPINGS

60 g (2 oz) vegan caramel sauce (page 142)

Mini vegan gingerbread men

100 g (4 oz) red currants

Vanilla Berry Christmas Cake with Cookie-Butter Filling

I absolutely love it when I get to bake and decorate this cake because I feel like it just screams winter wonderland and all things festive! I adore how it looks like a little snowy paradise and will add an extra-special finishing touch to any dinner table. The cake itself is made from two layers of delicate vanilla and cinnamon sponge cake with a spiced cookie buttercream filling and vibrant berry jam just waiting to ooze out the middle! The entire cake is encased in this glorious layer of vanilla bean and cinnamon frosting complete with sugared berries and baby meringues!

Preheat your oven to 355°F (180°C) and line two 6-inch (15-cm) cake pans with parchment paper.

To make the vegan buttermilk alternative, add the apple cider vinegar to the soy milk, stir and let thicken for 5 minutes.

Using a wooden spoon, cream together oil and sugar until pale and fluffy. To the same mixing bowl, add the buttermilk and vanilla and stir to combine.

Sift the flour, baking powder and baking soda and fold these into the wet ingredients with the cinnamon and nutmeg. Once you're left with a smooth cake batter, divide it evenly between the pans and bake for approximately 30 minutes.

Once the cakes are beautifully risen and golden, remove them from the oven and allow them to cool on a wire rack.

(continued)

Yield: 8–10 Servings

CAKE

15 ml (1 tbsp) apple cider vinegar

220 ml (7.5 oz) soy milk

90 ml (6 tbsp) olive oil

185 g (⅞ cup) superfine or granulated sugar

1 tsp vanilla bean paste

240 g (1⅞ cups) self-rising flour

5 g (2 tsp) baking powder

⅓ tsp baking soda

1 tsp ground cinnamon

Pinch of nutmeg

Vanilla Berry Christmas Cake with Cookie-Butter Filling (Continued)

Meanwhile, prepare the filling and frosting. For the cookie-butter filling, begin by using an electric hand whisk or stand mixer to beat the butter until pale and fluffy. This should take 3 to 5 minutes.

Gradually add the powdered sugar, Biscoff spread and cinnamon until everything is fully combined and the frosting is smooth and glossy.

To make the cinnamon frosting, beat the butter using an electric hand whisk or stand mixer for 2 to 3 minutes, until pale and fluffy. Gradually add the powdered sugar and cinnamon while continuing to mix until smooth and creamy.

To assemble, spread a layer of the cookie-butter filling over one of your cakes and pipe a ring of frosting around the edge. Fill the center with the jam and carefully place the second cake layer on top.

Coat the entire outside of the cake in cinnamon frosting and use a cake scraper and spatula to smooth this over for an even finish.

To decorate, arrange the red currants, cinnamon sticks and mini meringues around the edge of the cake and sprinkle with some cinnamon sugar to finish.

FILLING

120 g (½ cup) vegan stick butter

190 g (⅞ cup) powdered sugar

2 tbsp Lotus Biscoff spread

½ tsp ground cinnamon

60 g (4 tbsp) raspberry or mixed-berry jam

FROSTING

200 g (⅞ cup) vegan stick butter

260 g (1 ¼ cups) powdered sugar

¾ tsp ground cinnamon

TOPPINGS

150 g (5 oz) red currants

Cinnamon sticks

Vegan mini meringues

Cinnamon sugar

Acknowledgments

I'm so grateful that I've had the opportunity to write this book and share some of my favorite baking recipes with you in something that you can have yourselves at home! I feel so lucky to have been given this opportunity and want to say a massive thank-you to everyone who has supported me on this journey and follows my blog and social media. I would never have been able to do any of this without support from you, and I'm just so happy that you enjoy my recipes and content!

Thank you to my Mum for always being my biggest supporter throughout this journey from the very beginning! From pouring chocolate sauce over brownies for that perfect shot to keeping me calm and focused daily, I am forever grateful! I would never have been able to do this without you! I'll always appreciate the passion and support you've shown in Charley's Health. I couldn't have asked for more!

Thank you to all my incredible friends and family who have been so supportive during this process and have had to listen to cake-based conversation for the past three months. A very special thank-you also to everyone who has kindly stepped in as professional cake testers, especially my brother James. I'm so thankful for you testing pretty much each and every cake in this book and all of your help and support over the years! I hope the job wasn't too tasking and that you haven't become sick of cakes just yet!

Thank you to Becca for always being there to talk through and listen to my ideas, even the ridiculous ones! A massive thank-you for tolerating all my cooking chaos in our kitchens over the years and the excessive amount of equipment and ingredients that took over the kitchen cupboards! I couldn't ask for a better friend.

Thank you to Oli for always being there no matter the hour and for your endless support. Thank you also for being a constant voice of calm and reason whenever I'm chaotic and eating an endless number of cakes in the name of recipe testing!

A massive thank-you everyone at Page Street Publishing for giving me this incredible opportunity and allowing this book to come to life. A big thank-you to my editor, Madeline, for being such an incredible help with every stage of this process!

About the Author

Charlotte Roberts is the food blogger, photographer and recipe developer behind the Charley's Health blog. Charlotte grew up with a strong passion for both cooking and food in general and as a child always enjoyed helping her Mum bake cakes. She later developed a serious interest in plant-based food and loves exploring different alternative dishes and ingredients.

Charley's Health started as a platform for Charlotte to share her recipe experiments of healthier alternative and plant-based dishes with like-minded people. She adores helping people re-create classic recipe favorites and showing them that a vegan diet absolutely does not mean compromising on taste! This focus has since developed into a love for baking and creating decadent sweet treats with a plant-based twist. Charlotte always seeks to craft recipes that taste just as good (if not better) than the originals and are enjoyable to make. She believes that delicious food should be enjoyed by everyone, and following a plant-based diet does not mean having to miss out on dessert!

When Charlotte's not cooking or taking photographs of food, she can be found with her dog, Bear, by her side. Charlotte loves being active and rarely sits still! She enjoys exploring new restaurants and spending time with family and friends, which of course frequently involves serving lots of food. Although Charlotte loves living and spending time in the city, she adores animals and being in nature with them, especially in an environment that involves sea life and being in the water!

Index